Walking TCU

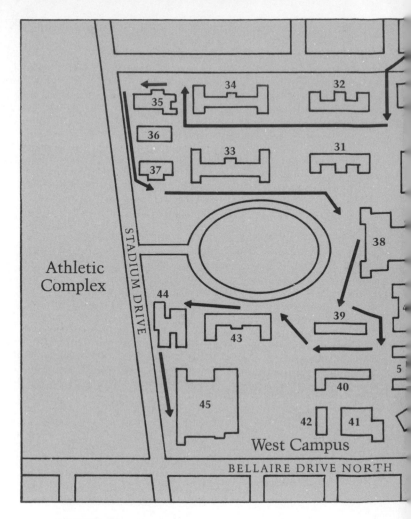

TCU Campus

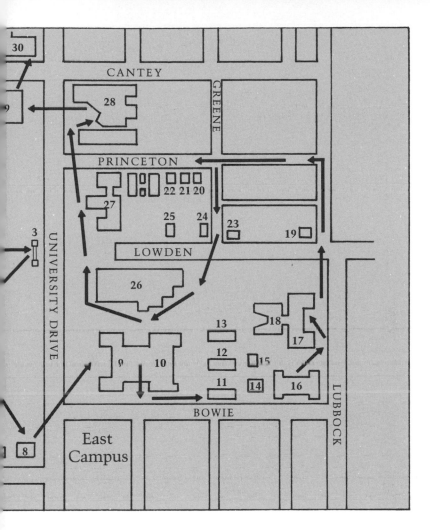

Athletic Complex & Worth Hills

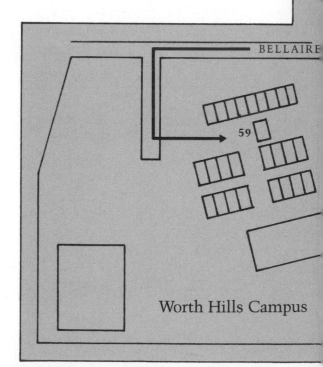

BELLAIRE

59

Worth Hills Campus

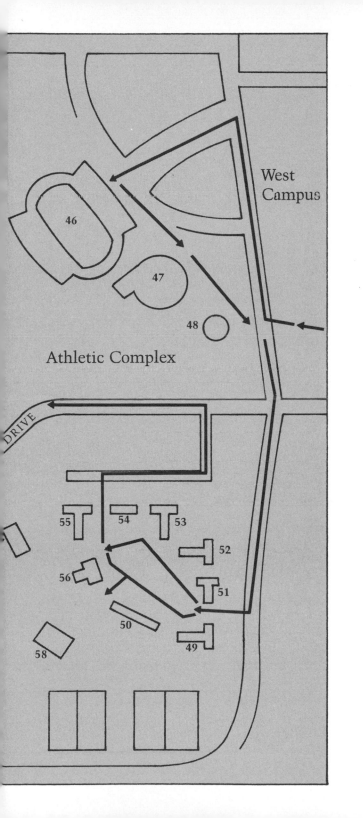

Joan Hewatt Swaim

WALKING TCU

A Historic Perspective

Texas Christian University Press
Fort Worth

Library of Congress Cataloging-in-Publication Data

Swaim, Joan Hewatt.
  Walking TCU : a historical perspective / by Joan Hewatt
Swaim.
    p. cm.
  Includes bibliographical references (p.) and index.
  ISBN 0-87565-104-6 : $9.95
    1. Texas Christian University—Guide-books. 2. Texas
Christian University—History. I. Title.
LD5311.T383S93 1992
378.764'5315—dc20   91-38344
                                         CIP

Designed by Whitehead and Whitehead
Cover illustration courtesy Special Collections,
TCU Library, and Barbara Whitehead.

Contents

Acknowledgments

THE author wishes to acknowledge those who have made the necessary research for this publication not only fruitful but also pleasurable. Foremost among these are Don Palmer and his staff in Facilities Planning. Jim Pettigrew, John Carter, Richard Mason, Sue Copeland, and Don himself opened to me their well-organized files of plans and blueprints, shared with me their expert knowledge, and buoyed me with their unlimited interest in the cause.

Nancy Bruce of the Special Collections Department of the Mary Couts Burnett Library never flagged in her support and supplied me with difficult-to-find documents and photographs pertinent to the TCU story. Roger Rainwater and Laura Dubiel of the same department were also very helpful.

Harrell Moten, TCU Director of Publications, has literally piles of photographs which he allowed me to sift through; Gerald Saxon in the Special Collections Department at the University of Texas at Arlington Libraries accorded me the same courtesy.

To my manuscript readers for their valued opinion, advice, and encouragement, my heartfelt thanks.

These are friend and confidante, Mary Lu Schunder;
friend and son, Mike Swaim; friend and daughter,
Susie Kurtz.

And there were so many others who willingly
spent time with me and told me what I needed to
know: Sara Bartzen, Dorothy Blackwell, Bettye Bois-
selier, Joe Britton, Bita May Hall Compton, Laura Lee
Crane, Chuck Dowell, Ray Drenner, Arthur
Ehlmann, Joe Enochs, Kelly Erwin, Lynn Evans, Mary
Charlotte Faris, Ellen Page Garrison, Joyce Harden,
Helen Huskey, Steve Kentigh, Sarah Normand
Kerner, Henri Etta Kilgore, Herbert LaGrone, Suzette
Lomax, Mason Mayne, Don Mills, Andy Paquette,
Mildred Payne, Libby Proffer, Dwayne Simpson, Em-
met and Judy Smith, Darla Smith, Wilma Miller
Smith, Kim Spinks, and Andy Williams.

I also turned, as I so often do, to Johnny Swaim
and to the "resident memory" mom, Elizabeth
Hewatt, for stories, facts, and dates, as well as pa-
tience and forbearance.

And finally, gratitude must be expressed to my
"boss," Library Director Fred M. Heath, and to my
nigh-on-to-perfect staff, who put up with my less-
than-full attention to library matters so that I might
work on this project.

Walking TCU:
A Prologue

THE land was yet prairie when they came, the
hill rising up to the southwest from the Clear Fork of
the Trinity River bottom, still rough and untidy with
shrubby brush, grasses, and wild flowers. Jackrabbits,
coyotes, and Texas horned lizards still held the terri-
tory. Dairies and ranches had been established here,
but the land was hardly approachable — not yet
tamed, not yet campus, not yet even a part of the
city, the center of which lay some three miles dis-
tant toward the northeast.

They had come, in that summer of 1910, on a
promise, and with a far vision and a dream, leaving
the burnt-out shell of an earlier dream standing
amidst its ruin in Waco to the south. Fort Worth had
promised fifty acres on which to begin again and
$200,000 with which to start. In addition, the city
would provide utilities, trolley line access, and inclu-
sion in its boundaries. It was an offer they could not
refuse.

So they had come. Two of their number, the Clark
brothers, had set out from Fort Worth thirty-seven
years before, to pursue yet an earlier dream of estab-

ACCEPTED LAYOVT - TEXAS CHRISTIAN VNIVERSITY

Chalmers McPherson
(courtesy Mary Couts
Burnett Library).

lishing a strong, lasting institution dedicated to education within the context of a Christian way of life, believing that enlightenment was the sure way to salvation. Their ideals had been taken up by men and women of similar vision, and it would be they who would water the tree of education, the tree of what the 1887 catalogue called "unperishable riches," to be transplanted for a third and final time now on this Texas hilltop.

In January 1911, the school newspaper published a preliminary sketch of the new Texas Christian University campus as envisioned by prominent Fort Worth architects, Waller & Field. An accompanying article by Reverend Chalmers McPherson, the university's endowment secretary, explained:

2

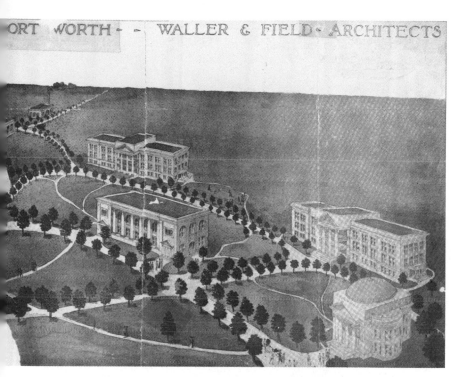

Artist's sketch of "accepted layout" of the Fort Worth campus, December 1910 (courtesy Mary Couts Burnett Library).

The Skiff gives to its readers this week a picture of the "Lay-out" of the new T.C.U. This picture is, in part, a dream. The dream is one, however, which will come to pass in the future. A goodly part of it is coming to pass now. . . .

The reason for adopting the ground plans for so many buildings at present is that there may be perfect harmony in the arrangement. The grounds should be properly laid out and every building which is expected to be erected in the future should have its proper place assigned to it.

The sketch includes ten buildings. "So many buildings . . . ," "perfect harmony in the arrangement . . . ," "every building which is expected to be erected in

3

Scene at the Administration Building cornerstone
ceremony, May 9, 1911 (courtesy Mary Couts Burnett
Library).

. . . its proper place. . . ." Visions can extend just so
far.

The "accepted layout" was altered only slightly by
the time foundations were laid for the two initial
structures, an administration building and a girls'
dormitory. Let under one contract to the Texas Building Company, both were to be ready for use at the
opening of the fall term that September. Another dormitory, to house men and ministerial couples, was
on the drawing board and it, too, would be completed
by the start of the 1911 semester.

With the car line still a mile and a half away, a
cornerstone-laying ceremony was planned for May 9,
1911, to coincide with the twenty-fifth annual assembly of the Texas Christian Missionary Convention, an organization that followed the teachings of
Alexander Campbell and his doctrine of non-denomi-
national "Disciples of Christ." It was to be a day
given over entirely to university interests and was

4

advertised in the *Skiff* as a "real jubilee day." An invitation was issued to the public, and a call went out for as many as had automobiles or any other vehicles to meet at the end of the Summit Avenue car line to aid in conveying out to the campus and back those celebrants who would take the trolley from town. (In early 1911, the car line probably ended at Eighth Avenue and Weatherbee Street.) With some walking, some motoring, and some riding in buggies and wagons, they made their way across the bare, rough fields toward the two buff-yellow brick structures standing partially finished, solitary in a sea of Johnson grass as far as the eye could see. A crowd of 2000 gathered near the temporary stage erected at the northeast corner of the main building, bedecked for the occasion with purple and white streamers. They stood on the ground amongst the sand heaps and rubble, leaned from windows, and hung from the construction scaffolding to gain a vantage point from which to witness the ceremony that included a parade of the student body, faculty, and trustees. The band played, the glee club sang, and the students cheered. Speeches were made by representatives of church, community, and college, and finally the cornerstone, with its box of relics inside, was formally laid.

The previous year, Texas Christian University's first in Fort Worth, the school had operated from several leased buildings in temporary quarters downtown. Church and school officials, faculty and students were eager for the move onto their own land and into their own home, at least for the ten years they had promised to stay. The town seemed eager, too, to support its new university, and hurried to complete the laying of wires, pipes, and car tracks out to the grounds.

The ten years pledged were followed by ten more and then tens more. The city made good its promise of incorporation, and streets were cut, gravelled, paved, named and renamed. Streetcars came and went. Trees were planted, Johnson grass and, eventually, the wildflowers gave way to cultivated lawns and flower beds. Quiet neighborhoods formed on campus peripheries, bringing with them churches and schools. Businesses followed and flourished. The jubilation that had come with birth and new beginnings seasoned and settled.

In time, the new buildings of 1911 became, if they survived, the old buildings of 1991. The harmony which Chalmers McPherson deemed essential was continued for long in both placement of new buildings and in the use of the buff brick that would become known as "TCU brick." So well does most of the campus harmonize, that a cursory look does not quickly discern early from late. Upon closer inspection, however, architectural style differs, weathering shows, and subtle seaming appears, where old conjoins new.

If you want to steep yourself in TCU fact and history, a bibliography is provided from which you can read about how the brothers Clark — Addison and Randolph — opened their little school in 1869, in Fort Worth, only a village then on a limestone bluff above the Trinity. You can read about the removal of their Male and Female Seminary from the rough Hell's Half Acre section of the Fort Worth of the 1870s to the peaceful little community of Thorp Spring that lay some fifty miles to the southwest. You can read about how the school was founded there in 1873 and chartered in 1874 as Add-Ran Male and Female College, and how, in 1889, the college was presented to the Christian Churches of Texas, who accepted the challenge of its continuance. In pictures and words you will find the stories of the growing school's move, in 1895, to Waco, a city ninety miles south of Fort Worth, and of its final name change, in 1902, to Texas Christian University; how the main building, and thus the main school, burned there in 1910, precipitating the events — the offers, counselings, discussions, and contracts — that led to its final move, back to Fort Worth. You will find accounts of how the first buildings were begun on this Texas prairie hill in 1911, and how one thing led to another until the small college-become-university now occupies 243 acres of land, has a faculty and support staff of over 1500, and a student body of some 7000.

If you want a deeper sense of place and value, however, take this campus walk with me — perhaps on an early fall morning, when the air is crisp and the light is soft, and before the distraction of people and cars has taken over. Observe the commemorative plaques embedded in the sidewalks, the cornerstones on the buildings, the names on the buildings and consider who Colby Hall, Winton and Scott, Shelburne, and Sadler, and Waits, and Beckham, and Brite, and Meyer, and Moudy, and Neeley were and

7

are, and what they did to be so honored. Enter the restored 1925 reading room of the Mary Couts Burnett Library and descend the worn marble steps to a lower floor, where a large portion of the million-plus volumes are stored, and think about how many have passed there in search of the knowledge an academic library houses. Sit in the elegant simplicity of Robert Carr Chapel and listen to its carillon, as on the hour it plays the alma mater before tolling the time; sit in the stands of Amon Carter Stadium or Daniel-Meyer Coliseum and imagine being there when the home team wins and feel the pride in sweet victory; sit in Landreth Auditorium, conjure a convocation and savor the ceremony of academe; climb to the top level of the west stadium stand and look out over the campus to the east, pick out the remaining original buildings and see just how far we've come. Sit in the Faculty Center on the second floor of Reed Hall, and

8

Aerial view of TCU, about 1985 (courtesy Mary Couts Burnett Library).

if you know, you can sense the presence of the early administrators, faculty, and students of TCU, for this building was long the active heart of the campus, and this room was actually not a room, but the balcony of an auditorium below, an auditorium that served as chapel, concert hall, meeting place, and the stage for graduation exercises until 1949. For those of us who know, this room fairly rings with the eloquent tones of then-President E. M. "Prexy" Waits, quoting po-etry as he was wont to do while conducting chapel services, and it fairly rings with the strains of the alma mater sung by the congregation gathered for baccalaureate. Listen —

Hail, all hail, TCU
Mem'ries sweet, comrades true.
Light of faith, follow through.
Praise to thee, TCU

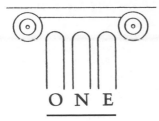

ONE

The Original Campus

JARVIS DORMITORY

THE tour begins, as the Fort Worth campus began, with Jarvis Dormitory and the early Administration Building, since become Dave Reed Hall.

Except for minor alterations, Jarvis' 1911 exterior remains unchanged. Waller & Field, leading Fort Worth architects of the early twentieth century, designed the dormitory in the Classical Revival style, featuring a flat roof fronted on the east by a central pedimented portico supported by four massive Ionic columns. The building is faced in the buff-yellow brick trimmed with cast stone that, with a few notable exceptions, distinguishes TCU buildings. In 1955, renovation removed the second- and third-story wooden galleries that were suspended between the central columns and the east wall of the building, and aluminum window frames replaced the earlier wooden ones. A 1989 survey conducted by the Historic Preservation Council of Tarrant County, Texas, considered that Jarvis could be "individually eligible" for the National Register of Historic Places "following the sympathetic rehabilitation of the windows."

Jarvis Hall, 1928 (author's collection).

Jarvis Hall, 1990 (courtesy University Publications).

One of the few surviving buildings of the pre-World War I campus, Jarvis is the only one that continues in the use for which it was built: to house women residents. Only twice in its past, and then for very brief periods, were the rooms occupied by men. From September 1942 to January 1944, men attending the World War II flight instruction programs being taught on the campus were housed in Jarvis, while the girls were moved into the newly built Foster Dormitory. Then, between 1950 and 1953, overcrowding dictated that Jarvis space be again temporarily assigned to male residents.

Jarvis is not only old in years, but its name also is venerable. Called simply the "Girls' Home" when built, it was soon named by vote of the Board of Trustees in honor of Major and Mrs. J. J. Jarvis, devoted and lifelong supporters of the university. Major Jarvis was a Fort Worth lawyer, businessman, and entrepreneur, whose interest in education was early evidenced by his advocacy of free public schools, an enterprise that met fierce opposition in the Fort Worth of the late 1870s and 1880s. When the infant forerunner of TCU had been relocated in Thorp Spring, Major and Mrs. Jarvis gave generously of their money and time to secure its mission. When Add-Ran College was chartered in 1889 as Add-Ran University (today spelled AddRan) under the control of the Christian Churches of Texas, Major Jarvis was elected the first president of the Board. He was responsible for expanding facilities provided by the one building at Thorp Spring, and one of the additions, "a four-story stone with seven good rooms," was known as "Jarvis Building."

Ida Van Zandt Jarvis, sister of General K. M. Van Zandt, without whose biography the history of Fort Worth cannot be told, was herself not only active but indeed influential in the affairs of TCU. An account written by Add-Ran alumna, Frankie Miller Mason, represents her as sympathetic to students, and one delightful story has her with white-flagged "truce" umbrella in hand confronting the president of the college, Addison Clark himself, on behalf of a large portion of the student body whose expulsion seemed imminent, all because of what she considered to be a slight infraction of the rules. The controversy was sparked by the discovery that a young male student had walked a young lady from the Thorp Spring campus to her home in the little town one evening, a strictly forbidden practice in 1882. In his defense, a large number of classmates owned up that they, too, had at one time or another violated that rule as well as others, whereupon Dr. Clark informed them all that they could consider themselves dismissed from the school. Mrs. Jarvis, viewing the punishment as too severe for the crime, made such a case that the president soon saw the absurdity in his rigid discipline, reportedly broke into laughter, and ended in not only pardoning the offenders, but also awarding them special privileges for a brief time.

By her own statement in an interview with Frankie Mason in 1935, it was Ida who authored the 1889 charter making Add-Ran College a university. In an

Ida Van Zandt Jarvis (courtesy Mary Couts Burnett Library).

Major J. J. Jarvis (courtesy Louise Burgess Logan).

1895 catalogue, she was listed as supervisor of the Girls' Home at Thorp Spring. In 1915, she was successful in having established the university's School of Home Economics, believing that every young woman should be taught how to sew and to cook. In 1931, she was the first woman elected to the Board of Trustees and served in that capacity until her death in 1937. Interestingly and appropriately, her place was filled by another woman, Sadie Beckham, who had since 1919 been the Jarvis Hall matron, supervisor of women, and later, dean of women. It was Mrs. Sadie who, as legend has it, each evening at seven, stood on the front steps of Jarvis ringing her cowbell to summon her charges into the fold for the night. In her time, young ladies living on the campus were not permitted out "after hours," nor to "date," nor to dawdle, and certainly not to dance.

Major and Mrs. Jarvis' eldest son, Van Zandt Jarvis, would continue his parents' support of the university, serving on the Board of Trustees for thirty-nine years, thirteen as the president. Two children of the Jarvis' other son, Daniel, were both graduates and long-time staff members at TCU, Dan as a professor of geology and Ann Day Jarvis McDermott as special collections librarian.

As you enter Jarvis Hall, on the right is a small parlor. More spacious and elegantly appointed in its youth, it was the school's sole accommodation for social affairs until 1942, when a larger, more modern room was provided by the new women's dormitory, Foster Hall. In addition to the festive teas and faculty receptions regularly hosted here, the Jarvis parlor provided women residents a place to entertain their friends and beaus — under the watchful eye of the hall matron. It was also used for more somber occasions, such as the funeral service in 1923 for my grandfather Frank L. Harris, the university's first steward of a cafeteria-style dining hall.

In the three floors above the high basement are

eighty rooms designed for double occupancy. The 1955 renovation included the installation of central air-conditioning, new bathroom fixtures throughout, additional storage and study space, as well as modern kitchen facilities, to make it one of the most desirable residences to coeds of that time. During the same renovation, the parlor was also refurbished; the Norwegian rose marble hearth and ash mantle and chair rails date from this period.

As you make your way out of Jarvis south to Reed Hall, pause for a moment between the buildings and recall the honeysuckle arbor that once covered the short walk from the south portico of Jarvis to the north Reed entrance. In a less multitudinous time, the arbor, with its sweet-smelling blossoms, served as the backdrop for outdoor graduation exercises held for many years on the lawns just east of the walk. There was rumor, too, that couples enjoying early socials called promenades (remember, *no* dancing!) would find its dark foliage a protection from ever-vigilant chaperones. The arbor was removed in 1948 because, according to one *Skiff* report, its "vines were beginning to die," and it had become "a trash catcher." A planned replacement never came to fruition.

DAVE C. REED HALL

THE way south from Jarvis leads to its companion in history, Reed Hall. It was at the northeast corner of this building that the first cornerstone on the Fort Worth campus was laid in 1911. Called simply the Administration Building until 1960, when Sadler Hall was built to house primary administrative units, it has since been named in honor of Dave C. Reed, Austin businessman, church leader, and university supporter who served on the TCU Board

Original Administration Building, framed by Memorial Arch, about 1945 (courtesy Mary Couts Burnett Library).

Dave Reed Hall and Memorial Columns, about 1952 (courtesy University Publications).

of Trustees from 1920 until his death in the crash of his private plane in Virginia in 1948. An honorary Doctor of Laws degree awarded Dave Reed in 1944 cited the TCU benefactor for his many contributions to the life of the university and referred to him as "a specialist in the finest of all arts — the art of living." Earlier, a two-story home on nearby Princeton Street that housed girl residents and later ministerial students had been named Reed Cottage. The "cottage" gave way long ago to an expanding campus community, but the old Ad Building endures to recognize the generosity of its namesake.

As with the Jarvises, Dave Reed was not the only member of his family to lend support to the university. His brother, Malcolm, had preceded him on the Board of Trustees from 1911 to 1919, and his son, Hiram, followed, serving from 1950 through 1959. Both also made significant financial contributions.

Although Reed Hall is now structurally joined on the west to the Brown-Lupton Student Center, the two are distinct functional units and will be treated as such on this tour.

Unlike Jarvis, Reed Hall has undergone extensive alterations — so many, in fact, that only long memory and old pictures can say how it was. Its original façade was a larger replica of Jarvis, with six Ionic columns supporting a shallow gable roof that projected over the central entrance veranda. Crosspaned double wooden doors bore brass doorplates enhanced with reliefs of the university's official mascot, the Horned Frog.

In the 1960 renovation design of architect Joseph Pelich, the original classical architecture was transformed into neo-Georgian; the six columns were removed, the formerly flat roof was restructured into a hip-style overall, and the wide front steps were replaced by stairs mounting on each side to a red-tiled terrace, railed with wrought metal and cast stone. Three sets of double aluminum-and-glass doors replace the wooden entrance, and the brass frog plates gave way to aluminum also.

But the past, as pasts do, still persists and can be discovered, when you know where to look for it. If you stand on the sidewalk just near either corner of the front steps and let your eye follow up high along the drain pipe, you can see where the bricks of now join the bricks of then, the newer not quite as seasoned and yellowed by time as the older, smoother brick. Real old-timers will recall that ivy once covered the walls, even to the roof.

Inside, the worn-down concrete steps between the floors have been treaded with vinyl, wooden hand rails have been replaced with metal, and the ground floor of the old auditorium has all but disappeared into a series of offices, seminar rooms, and a large meeting room. For those who rummage for remnants, stairs that once mounted to the auditorium stage wings from the left can still be seen, in new guise, at the southwest corner of Room 109, and the high reaches of that same stage form a strange recess in the far west wall of the second-floor Faculty Center.

Throughout its long history, the Administration Building – Reed Hall has provided space for classrooms and faculty offices; nearly every academic program on the campus began instruction in this building. It has also been, at various times, home to university presidents and vice-presidents, and once housed the library, the business and registrar offices, the post office, the university bookstore, the kitchen and dining room, the student lounge, and, for thirty-eight years, the only room large enough for campus assembly of any size — the old auditorium. Named Townsend Hall, after its smaller predecessor on the Waco campus which was so-named in honor of the S. E. Townsend family of Midland, the auditorium was variously used for chapel and church services, theatrical productions, graduation services, and student programs and presentations of all types.

Dave C. Reed (courtesy Mary Couts Burnett Library).

Reed Hall now has twelve classrooms and two seminar rooms, and it provides office space for the administrative staff of AddRan College of Arts and Sciences and for the humanities faculties of English, history, geography, and modern languages. AddRan College is the oldest and largest of TCU's academic units, a school of the university which retains a portion of the initial name of Add-Ran Male and Female College.

The Faculty Center occupies the west central extension on the second floor of Reed. Formerly the galleried balcony of the old auditorium, it was floored and remodeled into a large lounge area in 1955. Carpeted and handsomely furnished with comfortable seating, drapes, and decorative objects, it has since been used as a faculty club and luncheon room. It is not limited, however, to this function and is regularly in use by the Faculty Senate, for ROTC officer induction ceremonies, special lectures, afternoon teas, and, occasionally, for wedding receptions.

A museum occupies a small room to the right as you enter the Faculty Center. Among the treasures of the "Clark Room" are two antique desks used by the Randolph Clarks, articles of antique clothing, including the wedding dress of Mrs. Randolph (Ella) Clark, and Randolph's Bible. In addition, there are large portraits of Addison, Randolph, and Joseph Lynn Clark, son of Randolph and Ella.

On the wall just outside the museum is a portrait

of the first director of the center, Mary Elizabeth
Waits Scott Williams. Her contributions to the life of
TCU, however, had a much wider range than that of
hostess of the Faculty Center. The daughter of President E. M. Waits, she was her widowed father's official hostess for university functions — even after her
marriage to geology professor Gayle Scott — up until
the time of Dr. Waits' retirement. Widowed herself
by the untimely death of Dr. Scott, she was on the
English faculty for many years and later married Cecil B. Williams, late chair of the English department.
Truly a "first lady of TCU," she was given an honorary doctorate in 1974, in recognition of her service
and devotion.

The Faculty Center also houses the Flora Rupe
Mills Collection of Old Glass. Started by Mrs. Mills
as a hobby, the collection contains some 2780 pieces
of early American pressed glass, blown glass, art
glass, cut glass, china, and porcelain. It has been
beautifully housed in lighted cases around the walls
and stage of the Faculty Center and has been cata-
loged in a handsome volume, *Old American Glass*,
which is on hand in the Faculty Center for those in-
terested in examining the glass in detail.

In their eighty years, the old walls of Reed have
witnessed much of the university's history. In 1918,
it survived an airplane collision at its northeast para-
pet. The young pilot, who was buzzing his girlfriend
in Jarvis Hall, was thrown from the single-engine
machine and landed, unhurt, on the honeysuckle arbor below. In addition to the vast numbers of matric-
ulates who have walked its halls, it has also been
visited by celebrities, including American poets Carl
Sandburg, Robert Frost, and Vachel Lindsay, and once
played host to the orator, William Jennings Bryan,
and renowned pianist, Ignace J. Paderewski.

And, perhaps not quite as famous, there was the
cow, who, with the help of pranksters, somehow

found its way into President Waits' office and spent the night there. One story has it that, although the unfortunate creature was quickly removed upon discovery the next morning and the area thoroughly cleaned, a distinct "essence de bovine" persisted in the southeast corner on the first floor for many days. A later, and longer, residence was established in the early 1950s by an old stray dog that was adopted by the student populace and clandestinely allowed to sleep in the basement student lounge. So highly regarded was the "Old White Cawlie Dawg" that he won every student election for several years as a write-in candidate until he, as the cow before him, faced inevitable expulsion.

MEMORIAL COLUMNS AREA

Exiting the front entrance of Reed, go straight east along one of the parallel walks leading to University Drive and the Memorial Columns. Along these paths — the oldest on the campus — you can pause and ponder a past still perceptible to those who have been here before and still accessible even to the first-time visitor. Here, the shrubs and trees are older, the concrete cooler, and even though it runs close by, the buzz of busy University Drive seems less intrusive than elsewhere on this west side of the campus.

Those who come now from the years before 1949 will look in vain for a small, concrete vine-covered bandstand, an early landmark that stood on the lawn to the north of the esplanade. Once a band did play on it, while girls and their beaus walked around the campus grounds during the danceless "proms," and once pageants were staged and cheerleaders cheered from its platform. Slowly falling into disuse and crumbling into disrepair, it was removed when this side of the campus was graded and University Drive widened.

Whichever way you choose to approach the columns — the north or the south-running walk — you will notice marble plaques embedded in the concrete. An early tradition held that each graduating class, on parting, would present a gift to the university, in appreciation and commemoration of their time within its halls of learning. For several years, donated monies purchased portions of sidewalk paving for the campus; to note such gifts, the class would have a plaque, with members' names engraved, set into the stretch of walk for which they had paid. Over the years, needed campus improvements have left little evidence of the commemoratives, but we can still see some and say a little of what and where they were. Other gifts, gone in substance now but within still-active memory, included a masonry gateway from a Cantey Street entrance to the campus, a flagpole and a sundial situated across the walk opposite the bandstand, and a decorative stone flower urn-bench. Given in memory of English professor Walter E. Bryson the bench stood just east of the flagpole. Nothing remains of the gateway or the original flagpole area, and only plaques that accompanied the sundial and the Bryson Memorial remain. The sundial's bronze tablet with names of the class of 1927 lies in the grass at the fork in the walks between Reed and Sadler Halls. The small marble plaque from the Bryson urn lies in the north walk between Reed and the columns. All other sidewalk plaques — four near the columns and one each in front of the Bailey Building and on the west walk by the library — are believed to be those for which a portion of paving was paid.

The Memorial Arch that originally stood near where the freestanding Memorial Columns are today was itself a gift of the Class of 1923, presented in honor of the students and alumni who paid the supreme price in World War I. The original memorial was a flat bricked arch supported by brick piers and limestone Ionic columns. The span forming the arch was embellished with an entablature containing relief panels of an eagle and cartouches. The arch was the design of Clyde Woodruff of the architectural firm of Van Slyke & Woodruff. By 1949, when University Drive was widened and the arch was relocated and reconstructed into the present columns, there had been another war, and more dead heroes, so the new memorial was dedicated to them all.

The columns are made of Indiana limestone; the expanse between the columns is of Carthage stone. The names of the dead from World Wars I and II are inscribed on bronze plaques on the east front of the memorial, and the names of the 1923 seniors are listed on a similar bronze tablet on the west side.

Retracing your steps west toward Reed, you will pass the Shirley Boyd Memorial Garden, planted in the midsection of the grassy mall between the parallel walks. In the growing seasons, this plot, given by a history professor in memory of his wife, is bright with blooms of tulip, pansy, petunia, and daisy.

As you skirt around the southeast corner of Reed, on your way to Sadler Hall, the Horned Frog will surely catch your eye. Commissioned by the 1984 Student House of Representatives, styled and cast in metal by artist Seppo Aarnos, it has become one of the campus' favorite landmarks. Something about the cocky tilt of its head captures and commands comment from resident and visitor alike. It was likely just such a proud specimen of the live variety of the Texas horned lizard that inspired its adoption as school mascot in 1896, when the school was in Waco. The frog occupies a portion of the student outdoor commons that spans the area between Reed and Sadler halls and borders the southeast entrance to the Brown-Lupton Student Center.

SADLER HALL

THE stately building that is M. E. Sadler Hall houses the chief administrative and business units of the university. Designed by Preston M. Geren and completed in September 1960 at a cost of $1.2 million, it is the second structure to occupy this site. In 1912, a men's dormitory was erected here as the fourth building on TCU's Fort Worth campus; it was named Clark Hall in honor of the school's founders. By 1959, the older building was in such a deteriorated condition that it was deemed unsalvageable and was demolished to provide space for the new administration building. The old Administration Building was renovated into the classroom and office facility now known as Reed Hall.

Built during the administration of Chancellor Mac-Gruder Ellis Sadler, the present four-story structure was named Sadler Hall by the Board of Trustees in recognition of the long and successful service of the man chosen in 1941 to guide the university's fortunes. Having distinguished himself as a student leader at Atlantic Christian College, Vanderbilt, and Yale, where he was awarded the B.D. and Ph.D. degrees, he was first the dean of Lynchburg College, then minister of the Central Christian Church in Austin, Texas. At the time of his appointment as president of Texas Christian University (the title of the chief executive officer was changed to chancellor

M. E. Sadler Hall, 1989 (courtesy University Publications).

McGruder Ellis Sadler
(courtesy Mary Couts
Burnett Library).

in 1959), eight buildings stood on the campus. Upon his retirement in 1965, twenty-one new buildings had been erected and five existing structures had been renovated and/or enlarged. The quarter-century Sadler era would be noted for this unequalled campus expansion, as well as for strong and steady guidance. His vision and wisdom are attested to on nearly every page of the institution's history during those years, and his influence is felt to the present day. Upon his death in 1966, his friend, protégé, and successor, Dr. James M. Moudy, gave this valediction: "A mighty oak has fallen and a thousand seeds have scattered."

The design of Sadler Hall combines some of the elements of the early campus architecture with later construction characteristics. The color scheme of buff brick and red-toned roofing is continued, as is the use of tall columns — this time with Corinthian capitals — that support a gabled portico over a wide, stepped entrance veranda. A traditional campus Christmas program takes place before these portals, with students, staff, faculty, and administrators joining in the singing of carols and the lighting of a giant evergreen.

In the central foyer of Sadler Hall, a gallery displays a large oil painting of Dr. Sadler as well as a bronze bust — a remarkable likeness of the educator, sculpted by Electra Waggoner Biggs. It was commissioned and presented to the university by friends of the late chancellor. Also on view in the gallery, which was provided in 1991 by Chancellor and Mrs. William E. Tucker, are pictures depicting buildings and scenes of TCU past and present. A bronze outline of the university seal is set in the terrazzo floor, a gift of the Classes of 1961 and 1962.

The first and ground floors of Sadler Hall now accommodate the business, admissions, and registrar offices, the student affairs complex, student financial aid, printing and mailing facilities, and the post office. The upper two floors house offices of the chan-

cellor, vice-chancellors, development staffs, public
relations, extended education, news service, and a
board room for meetings.

A caveat must be entered now into the text, for as
you leave by the front entrance of Sadler Hall, you
will need to stay on formally laid-out walks during
the remainder of your time on this southwesterly
portion of the campus. In the late '40s and most of
the '50s, this turf belonged to the Cowboy, and it's
rumored that it still belongs to his ghost. Cowboy
Monroe, one-time groundskeeper, was by far the
crustiest critter to roam this range. Armed with a
hefty garden hose and a whistle, his bowed legs stuck
into ancient boots and his wizened face topped with
an oversized cowboy hat, he was the enforcer of terri-
torial ground rules and wouldn't hesitate to fire a
well-aimed water volley from his hose toward any-
one — student, professor, or chancellor — who dared
to step onto "his" grass. As you make your way,
then, from Sadler south to Clark Hall, forewarned is
forearmed!

CLARK HALL

THE name of this present men's dormitory is a
legacy, appropriately handed down to mark and hold
a place of honor for the Clark name in the university's story. When Sadler was built on the original
Clark Hall site, the name was passed south to the
new building, which itself supplanted a former residence hall called Goode, in honor of the primary do-
nor to its construction cost, Mrs. M. A. Goode of Bart-
lett, Texas. The Clark Hall of 1912 was so-named as
a "memorial" to the two brothers, Addison and Randolph Clark, founders of the university. Both brothers were living at the time of the announcement of
the proposed honor, and permission to use their

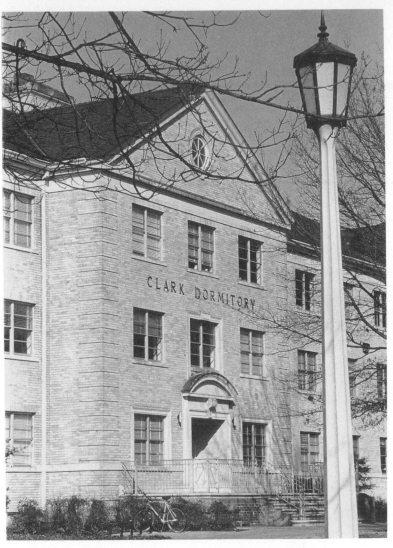

Clark Hall, about 1989 (courtesy University Publications).

name was granted after modest hesitation. Chalmers McPherson, endowment secretary, expressed the sentiment behind the proposition: "It is better, by far, to place flowers at the feet of the living than to strew them on the grave of the dead. . . . In harmony with this thought it occurred to some . . . to begin plans

Original Clark Hall (foreground) and Goode Hall, about 1940 (courtesy Mary Couts Burnett Library).

for a memorial to the brethren . . . Clark . . . while they were still among us." Within a week of this pronouncement, Addison was dead.

The present Clark Hall recognizes not just the brothers but their progenitors and descendants, as well. Joseph Addison Clark, Sr., and his wife, Hettie D'Spain Clark, took an active part in the founding of Add-Ran College in 1873 at Thorp Spring. A sister, Ida Clark Nesbit, and a younger brother, Tommy, also shared the family interest in the new school. Particularly important to TCU history is Joseph Lynn Clark, Randolph's son, who wrote the book entitled *Thank God We Made It!*, which documents his predecessors' dedication to the "unwearying dream,"

Joseph Addison Clark
(courtesy Mary Couts
Burnett Library).

Randolph Clark (courtesy
Mary Couts Burnett
Library).

Addison Clark (courtesy
Mary Couts Burnett
Library).

recounting the family's efforts and accomplishments
in the field of education. Professor Clark's papers,
including letters and family documents, are in the
Special Collections of the Mary Couts Burnett Library on the campus.

Before 1948, Clark and Goode were the only permanent structures that housed men. But old Clark
and old Goode were more than just student housing
units. Goode was built initially as a home to ministerial students and, very early in the school's Fort
Worth history, provided living quarters for TCU staff

and faculty members and their families. Prior to 1952, all science departments of the university, at one time or another, were located in the dark, dank basements of either Goode, Clark, or the old gymnasium to the south. It will be remembered, too, that old Clark Hall was turned over to the Navy V-12 training unit between 1943 and 1945. Other quarters were found for the war-diminished civilian male student population, "for the duration."

Always, as now, the wide expanse of flat, nearly treeless land that stretches from the walk in front of the present Clark Hall toward the western boundary of University Drive invited the young to play out their energies. Pictures and old-time memory recall the tennis courts that once were here, and each warm Texas day of the years since their removal has witnessed made-up games of volleyball, touch football, lacrosse, and, more recently, frisbee-throwing. Of course, while the ubiquitous groundskeeper, Cowboy Monroe, was on duty, one either had to pick cautiously his time for play or, as was often the case with the boys, purposely tread on the forbidden grass, just to hear him holler and threaten to turn the "young whippersnappers" in.

The present Clark Hall was built in 1958, and with its "E" shape provides as much room as the former Clark and Goode Halls combined. Rooms are designed for double occupancy, and each is furnished with bunk beds and built-in desks and drawers. The architectural style of Clark follows that of other campus dormitories of that time period with its Georgian façade, the buff brick, red-tiled roof, and entrance veranda.

Early in its use, freshmen and sophomore men were assigned rooms in Clark, but there is no such distinction now. It is, however, primarily occupied by non-Greeks or those waiting for an opening in the fraternity dorms on the Worth Hills section of the campus.

Ballet Building, former gymnasium (courtesy University Publications).

BALLET BUILDING

DIRECTLY south of Clark Hall is the building that is home to the ballet and modern dance department of the School of Fine Arts. The only major structure on the campus that remains unnamed, it has become known simply as the Ballet Building. Its exterior style and tone reveal its age; inside, the walls, floors, and stairs tell of long use. Upon closer inspection, one begins to suspect that the building was not originally designed for dance.

It was, in fact, built in 1921 as a gymnasium, which was the center for all physical education activities until 1973, when the new Rickel Health and Physical Education Building was completed. Called in its youth "a magnificent edifice . . . that bids fair to develop into one of the most complete plants in the South, in point of both space and equipment," the old gym has since been both appraised as an antique and damned as "an architectural monstrosity." Each viewer brings his own measure of value. Although the interior of the Ballet Building has been extensively altered, the exterior appears to be intact and, according to the Tarrant County Historic Resources Survey, may be eligible for the National Register of Historic Places.

The multi-level structure was the original design of official TCU architects Van Slyke & Woodruff, the same firm that fashioned the Memorial Arch. The "little gym," as it came to be called after a larger barn-like field house was built in 1926, was constructed of the buff "TCU brick" and featured industrial steel sash windows and a flat roof with curved parapets on each side. The high basement contained classrooms and offices; the swimming pool, men's and women's locker rooms, and more offices occupied the entrance level; a basketball court with a spectator balcony was on the third floor, as were two handball courts; the topmost floor eventually housed a weight room.

In addition to the physical training curriculum, TCU's athletic programs were directed from these halls prior to the construction of the Daniel-Meyer Coliseum in 1961. It was from a central office on the gym's main floor — now a conference room — that legendary football coach "Dutch" Meyer dreamed the plans and plotted the plays that would make him and his "Fightin' Frogs" famous in the '30s and '40s. It was on the third-floor hardwood court that TCU basketball teams first competed in Southwest Confer-

moved in 1954 to a religion center on the east campus.

At the suggestion of then-President F. D. Kershner, Fort Worth architects Sanguinet and Staats patterned their design of the 1914 building after the College of the Bible in Lexington, Kentucky. Buff-yellow brick and cast stone were again primary materials, and a flat roof and Tuscan columns that still support the pedimented portico harmonized with the early campus architecture. There was, however, slightly more ornamentation on the structure than on the other four buildings. This can be seen in the rusticated masonry on the ground floor, the decorative cornices, and the sculpted stone emblem on the portico's pediment.

In 1958, after the religion programs had moved to new quarters, the old Brite College building was renovated under the direction of architect Preston Geren. A hipped red-tiled roof replaced the former flat one, the second story entrance was restructured to ground level, aluminum windows supplanted wooden ones, and air conditioning was added throughout. At that time, the building was renamed The Bailey Building; it has since been occupied by the School of Education.

The Bailey Building received its name through the generosity of the family of Mary Ann and Robert Bailey, West Texas pioneers who lived in Fort Worth for many years. Always friends and supporters of TCU, the Baileys' interest carried over to their children and grandchildren. A daughter, Nora Bailey Gee of San Angelo, was responsible for planning the memorial to her parents and gave substantially toward its construction. A portrait of Mrs. Gee is on view in the second-floor lounge.

TCU's education program has grown from its inception in 1909 as a small department within the AddRan College of Arts and Sciences to the status of a separate school, offering classes in elementary and

Brite College of the Bible, 1914 (courtesy Mary Couts
Burnett Library).

Bailey Building, 1989 (courtesy University Publications).

37

secondary education, as well as physical education and special education. Since its establishment in 1924, the School of Education has earned accreditation by the Texas Education Agency and the National Council of Accreditation of Teacher Education. Approval by the national council means that certificates granted by the school are recognized in many states other than Texas. TCU's education program is spread over the curriculum; majors and minors in AddRan College of Arts and Sciences, in music, and in nursing all include degree options with teacher certification.

Leaving the Bailey Building, to the east and across University Drive is the Winton-Scott Hall of Science. At the crossing, another glance back down through the tunnel of time is occasioned. From 1911 until 1923, the busy four-lane thoroughfare, now known as University Drive, was a dirt-and-gravel extension of Forest Park Boulevard, down the middle of which came the streetcar from Fort Worth, three miles to the north. The southern boundary of the campus, marked by the original Brite College building, was literally the end of the line. Only prairie lay farther south, and until the early '20s, an eastern horizon was unobstructed, as well. The sale of large tracts of land to real estate developers and a subsequent residential housing boom brought paved streets, businesses, churches, and public schools to the area. The strip of shops on the east side of University Drive across from the Bailey Building, long known as the "drag," was built during this time. On-campus student services, ready transportation, and shopping malls have diminished college "drags" to shadows of former days. The future of the TCU drag is fragile; one only has to remark the condition of the TCU Theatre at the south end of the row to sense the decline.

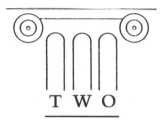

T W O

The East Campus

WINTON-SCOTT HALL OF SCIENCE

THE building of the Winton-Scott Hall of Science in 1952 brought instruction in all the sciences together under one roof for the first time in over thirty years. When the school opened its fall semester of 1911 on the new Fort Worth campus, the laboratory sciences were taught in the only building used then for instruction, the Administration Building (now Reed Hall). As each discipline grew, space was provided for the enlarged science programs in the basements of extant buildings. Soon, and for long, the old Clark dormitory was home to the combined biology/geology department, Goode Hall housed chemistry, and the physics department was located in the gymnasium, now the Ballet Building. The chemistry department made one more move to temporary buildings on the east campus before settling in to Winton-Scott.

Heralded in the *Skiff* as "one of the outstanding little science buildings in the United States," with facilities unsurpassed in the Southwest, the five-story structure was the design of architects Wyatt C. Hedrick, Preston M. Geren, and Joseph R. Pelich. Its

Winton-Scott Hall of Science, about 1989 (courtesy University Publications).

basic style follows that of other post-World War II campus buildings with buff brick and cast stone trim, red-tiled hipped roof, and a plain classical aspect. Aluminum was extensively used for decorative interest, as seen in the window spandrels, the grilles above the high cornice, and the cast aluminum central door grilles that carry representative symbols of the four major sciences the building initially housed: an amoeba for biology at upper left, the sun for physics at lower left, a geologic cross-section at upper right, and the apparatus of chemistry at lower right. The central entrance is set in relief by a dark polished granite facing, the first use of this material on

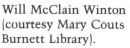

Will McClain Winton
(courtesy Mary Couts
Burnett Library).

Gayle Scott (courtesy Mary
Couts Burnett Library).

campus buildings. Four exterior sculptures — one
each of cast aluminum on the west front wings, and
one each of cast stone over the north and south entrance porticoes — are also symbolic of the use for
which the building was intended.

The science hall is the only academic building on
the campus named in honor of the faculty who ac-
tively contributed, through teaching and research, to
the programs housed within its walls. Professor Will
M. Winton and his protégé, Gayle Scott, were both
geologists, who had significant influence, not only
within the science curriculum at TCU, but also
within their chosen profession.

Professor Winton began his long tenure in 1913, as
chairman of the biology/geology department. He
never completed his doctorate at Rice Institute (now
Rice University), but his research in the field of geol-

ogy won him national recognition as a Fellow in the American Academy of Science. His Texas geologic survey maps proved of incalculable value in the early development of the petroleum industry in North Texas. National acclaim, as well as local renown as respected teacher and colleague, led the university in 1951 to bestow on him the honorary Doctor of Science degree.

Professor Winton was responsible for initiating two medical science programs at TCU that have envied reputations in the Southwest and continue to attract large numbers of undergraduates to their studies. The pre-medical program, approved from the outset by the American Medical Association, was begun in 1918; the medical technology program was begun in 1939. Winton chaired the pre-medical program from 1918 to 1950, two years before his retirement in 1952.

Gayle Scott was one of Professor Winton's first students, receiving his bachelor's degree in 1917 and his master's in 1920. After serving as an officer in the First World War, Dr. Scott pursued his studies in geology at the University of Grenoble, France, where he received his doctorate in 1925. A specialist in cretaceous geology, he compared cretaceous sediments of Texas with those of western Europe in his doctoral thesis, causing a mild controversy at the time; his hypotheses were later found to be correct. As Winton had before him, Scott became professionally involved at the national level as a publishing researcher and active participant in geologic societies, particularly the American Association of Petroleum Geologists and the Society of Economic Paleontologists and Mineralogists, serving as president of the latter in 1939. Married to the TCU president's daughter, Mary Elizabeth Waits, "Scotty," as he was affectionately known, had active interest in many aspects of the TCU world, but none more active than his participation in its athletic programs. He chaired the faculty

42

athletic committee from 1937 until 1948 and was president of the Southwest Conference Athletic Association. At the age of fifty-three and at the peak of his career, his life was cut tragically short by an inoperable brain tumor. Commemorative bronze plaques with relief portraits of Drs. Winton and Scott may be seen in the first-floor entrance foyer.

Winton-Scott Hall of Science currently houses the departments of biology, psychology, and mathematics, as well as TCU's military science programs. Worth a visit is the extensive marine shell collection displayed in lighted museum cases in the fourth-floor corridor. A gift of Mrs. Ruth F. Mudd, the collection is maintained by the Department of Biology.

SID W. RICHARDSON PHYSICAL SCIENCES BUILDING

ACCESS to the Sid W. Richardson Physical Sciences Building may be made by exiting either the north or the south entrances of Winton-Scott and walking east to the ramped walks leading to a courtyard and the front entrance. Alternatively, on the third and fourth floors of Winton-Scott, two elevated passages join the buildings and provide access to the corresponding floors in Richardson. Choosing the interior route guarantees more adventure; it is easy, even for campus veterans, to become lost in the labyrinthine halls and stairways of this structure that houses the physical sciences.

In many ways, the Sid W. Richardson was the most ambitious and certainly the most costly building to be added to the campus. Its construction, begun in 1968, was to complete a $7.6 million science research complex that included the conjoining of a remodeled Winton-Scott Hall. The plan was for the latter to quarter the life sciences and for the new building to house the physical sciences, as well as a computer center, which had been established in 1961 and housed in Rogers Hall. When the complex was completed, the space for instruction and research in the sciences at the university was more than tripled.

On the basement level, Sid W. Richardson is home to the Computer Center and Management Information Services. The complex currently houses two major computer systems and provides support for virtually all computerized operations on the campus — academic, research, and administrative. The departments of geology and environmental sciences are on the second level; physics, the Center for Remote Sensing and Energy Research, and the Department of Computer Science occupy the third level; the chemistry department is found on the fourth. A fifth floor, called the "penthouse" level, is occupied by the offices of university relations, publications, and editorial services. This topmost floor also accommodates a large meeting room, frequently used by the TCU Board of Trustees and by the Faculty Senate, and a seldom-used outdoor terrace.

The design of the Richardson building, conceived by renowned architect Paul M. Rudolph, was to some a drastic, unnecessary departure from traditional TCU style. To others, it was a work of art, a forward-looking, welcome break with the monotonous squared classical look of the past. Aware of the controversy, Rudolph, speaking at the cornerstone-laying ceremony, commented that the building looked to the traditional architecture of TCU and also to the future. He continued, "I know of no other university that has tried to house its best scientists in what is, hopefully, a work of art." According to Rudolph, each element of the building would be "clearly articulated." There would be no attempt to hide such interior necessities as columns and stairs. Ironically, by the early 1990s the open stairwell was in violation of fire codes. The university was directed to enclose all

44

Sid W. Richardson Physical Sciences Building, about 1980 (courtesy University Publications).

Sid W. Richardson (courtesy University Publications).

stairs, thus violating the aesthetic intent of the architect.

The Richardson building provides the school with six of its largest lecture halls. Each is built with amphitheater armchair seating. In the second-level entrance lobby, just off the courtyard, is a fine exhibit provided by the Department of Geology. Here is displayed a small portion of specimens from the Monnig Meteorite Collection, the largest such collection in the Southwest. Also displayed in this area and in cases along the north and south halls of the same floor are rocks, minerals, geodes, and fossils. The Hutton Room, located in the northeast corner of this floor and used for seminars, also has fine examples of meteorites and petrified wood. And, for a laugh, don't miss the "Arthur J. Ehlmann Collection of Bad Art: A Tasteless Retrospective" in the glassed case down the north hall.

The name of the science complex honors the foundation which granted the greater portion of construction funds. Speaking at the cornerstone ceremony in 1968, Perry R. Bass said that the grant fulfilled a promise made by his uncle, the late Sid Richardson (1891-1959), to do "something significant" for TCU. Richardson's fortune came through enterprises in oil, cattle, and land in early-twentieth-century Texas. His interests extended over a wide range, and his philanthropy is nowhere more evident than in the foundation's generous support of education. A bronze bust of the philanthropist sculpted by Electra Waggoner Biggs stands in the north entrance lobby.

Other significant contributors to the more than $7 million cost of the science center were the Amon G. Carter Foundation of Fort Worth, the Moody Foundation of Galveston, and the United States Department of Health, Education, and Welfare.

TEMPORARIES, TAGER, GREENHOUSE

ALONG the way to the Annie Richardson Bass Building, several one-story, unnamed structures house important university programs. First is the TCU Counseling Center in a wooden unit facing Bowie Street. This building, an old army barracks, was moved to the campus sometime in 1946 or 1947, along with sixteen others the university purchased from army camps at Brownwood and Abilene following World War II. Due to the large numbers of veterans reentering college, TCU experienced a sharp rise in enrollment and needed extra space for classrooms and dormitories. Four of the wooden structures were

46

placed behind the "little gym" on the west campus to house male students; the remaining thirteen were located in the same general area now occupied by the Counseling Center. In the early 1950s, as permanent quarters became available for the programs housed in the barracks, most of the locally dubbed "Splinter Village" had been removed. The thoroughly reconditioned Counseling Center is the only one that remains.

Next on the north, the sociology department occupies the first metal structure, and farthest north, in the second metal structure, is the Institute of Behavioral Research. The sociology department is an academic unit of AddRan College of Arts and Sciences. The Institute of Behavioral Research is a private, not-for-profit organization and functions as a separate academic unit of TCU. Established in 1962 by the late Professor Emeritus Saul B. Sells, IBR works in close collaboration with the Department of Psychology and other departments at TCU. A tribute to Dr. Sells is framed on the foyer wall of the institute.

Directly to the east of the Counseling Center and set back from the street is the TAGER TV Studio with its prominent communications tower. The acronym stands for the Association for Graduate Education and Research of North Texas, and its services provide academic television in cooperation with other institutions and industrial firms. TAGER offers graduate courses in most areas taught by faculty members from TCU, Southern Methodist University, University of Dallas, and the University of Texas at Dallas. Courses are presented over a closed-circuit television network, with talkback facilities between the remote classrooms and the instructor.

To the immediate north of the TAGER building and encompassed by a wooden fence is the biology department's greenhouse. Plants grown within are used in research and as materials for classroom instruction.

47

BASS BUILDING

THE Annie Richardson Bass Building follows the earlier Sid W. Richardson Building in architectural style with its curved "corners" and open stairwells, as well as the materials used in its construction. It comes as no surprise, then, that Preston Geren, who served as an associate to Paul Rudolph in the design of the Richardson Building, was principal architect for the Bass Building.

A common chord is also struck in the names of the two buildings. Annie Richardson Bass was Sid Richardson's sister and the wife of locally prominent physician, E. Perry Bass. Their son, Perry R. Bass, has long been director of the Richardson Foundation. Mrs. Bass was an active educational and civic leader.

Although the Sid W. Richardson Foundation was the principal source of funds for the structure, other significant support was secured from the Karl and Esther Hoblitzelle Fund of the Southwestern Medical Foundation of Dallas, the J. E. and L. E. Mabee Foundation of Tulsa, the U.S. Department of Health, Education, and Welfare, and Anne Burnett Tandy. Mrs. Tandy provided funding for the nursing college's learning resource center in honor of Fort Worth surgeon, W. Burgess Sealy.

The Bass Building houses one college of the university and three departments of the AddRan College of Arts and Sciences. The Harris College of Nursing is located on the second floor, the Department of Nutrition and Dietetics and the Department of Engineering occupy the ground floor, and the Department of Design and Fashion has facilities on the third.

The Harris College of Nursing began as a privately run school founded in 1912 by Fort Worth physician, Charles Houston Harris. It became Dr. Harris' dream to establish a college with a baccalaureate program in

Annie Richardson Bass
Building, about 1988
(courtesy University
Publications).

Annie Richardson Bass
(courtesy University
Publications).

nursing. In 1946, thirty-four years after its inception,
the nursing school became the Harris College of
Nursing affiliated with Texas Christian University.
Lucy Harris (no relation to Dr. Harris) was employed
as first organizer and dean of the college and served
in that capacity from 1946 until her retirement in
1967. In the words of her successor, Virginia Jarratt,
"the Harris College of Nursing owes its programs

49

and its reputation to the quality of leadership provided by Dean Lucy Harris during its early years."

Home economics was founded as a school of the university in 1915, with the active participation and encouragement of Ida Van Zandt Jarvis. Mrs. Jarvis believed that the art and skill involved in managing a home had a proper place in a college curriculum. Since then, the program has gone through several transformations. In 1924, the Department of Home Economics became a part of the College of Arts and Sciences. In 1951, four categories of courses were offered: foods and nutrition, textiles and clothing, family life, and vocational home economics education. Instruction in interior design was soon added. In its present configuration, there are two major degree-granting departments: design and fashion, and nutrition and dietetics. Family life is no longer a part of the curriculum.

On the far east end of the ground floor of the Bass Building is a large living-dining room flanked on the north and south by small, pleasantly landscaped patios. The comfortably furnished "Bass Living Room" is in considerable demand for meetings, lectures, and seminars, and is also used as a laboratory dining room for students enrolled in quantity foods courses.

An exhibit case just outside the living room is used by fashion design students, whose displays are always colorful and interesting.

ROGERS HALL, TANDY HALL

Just north of the Bass Building, the M. J. Neeley School of Business is housed in Dan D. Rogers Hall and Charles D. Tandy Hall. The eastern portion of the dual structure is Rogers, completed in 1957; the western portion is Tandy, ready for use in 1989. East and west main entrances, as well as north and south

Dan D. Rogers Hall, about
1970 (courtesy University
Publications).

Dan D. Rogers (courtesy
Mary Couts Burnett
Library).

side entrances, provide access to both buildings.

Wyatt C. Hedrick, the architect who designed the Winton-Scott Hall of Science (1952), was responsible for the Rogers plan, the exterior of which reflects campus architecture of its day. It bears a strong resemblance to Winton-Scott in its long rectangular lines and exterior cast-stone murals that depict the business world activities of management and production. These can be seen on the west fronts of either first-floor wings. The design of Rogers also continued the use of dark polished granite to frame the entrance portal. The building and annexation of Tandy Hall eliminated the original entrance granite, but the material remains in all exterior window spandrels and the cornerstone, situated at the southwest corner of the hall.

Among other still-functional features of the 1957 building are a then-state-of-the-art 150-seat auditorium equipped with screen and projection booth, and a spacious reading room which was dedicated in 1973 to the memory of Ike H. Harrison, the late long-time dean of the School of Business. The room, now called the Centennial Study Room of Delta Sigma Pi, is located in the far northeast corner on the ground floor. It provides a small business library which supplements more extensive holdings in the university library. On display here are a bronze bas relief of Dean Harrison and an oil portrait of Dan D. Rogers, for whom the hall is named. The departments of accounting, management, and marketing are located in Rogers Hall.

Charles Tandy Hall is in stark contrast, architecturally, to its companion building. However, as with the joining of the Winton-Scott and Richardson buildings, Kirk, Voich, and Gist, the Tandy architects, achieved a harmonious blend in spanning the thirty-two years from 1957 to 1989. Upon entering Tandy from any of the several approaches, one is immediately met with an expanse of glass, chrome, and brown brick-tile. The crisp, clean lines of the building and its appointments recall the business world and strongly resemble a bank. An open stairway with glass panels and chrome trim mounts through the center of the atrium to upper floors where more glass doorways lead to wood-paneled office suites furnished with wood, black leather, and chrome. Modern office equipment hums; cushioned carpets absorb extraneous sound. Through the glass doors of the dean's office suite on the third floor, a sweeping view of the mall leading from Tandy Hall west across University Drive to Sadler Hall is provided.

Tandy Hall houses the business school's Center for Productive Communication and the Charles Tandy American Enterprise Center. A computer laboratory and teleconferencing facilities are located here also.

As early as 1884 TCU had courses in business. Called then the Commercial School, its curriculum included "complete accounting," commercial arithmetic, and commercial law. Except for a brief period between 1886 and 1890, business studies have since been offered under various organizational names: the School of Business from 1896 to 1901; the College of Business from 1901 to 1922; and the Department of Business Administration from 1922 until 1938, when it again became the School of Business. In 1967, it was named the M. J. Neeley School of Business.

The three names with which the business complex is associated most appropriately label the two buildings and the school they house. Dan D. Rogers, M. J. Neeley, and Charles D. Tandy had unusual qualities that assured them of success as businessmen, and the university has been fortunate, indeed, to be recipients of their generous support.

It would be difficult to find a truer, more loyal and stalwart supporter of TCU than Dan D. Rogers, who throughout his adult life never wavered in his enthusiasm for his alma mater. A member of the Class of 1909, he was a band member, cheerleader, and class officer. Upon graduation, he was instrumental in organizing the alumni association and served as its first president in 1913. An avid sports fan, Rogers promoted the building of the first stadium on the Fort Worth campus, old Clark Field, whose wooden bleachers and steel stands were erected on land just west of where the Rogers-Tandy buildings are now located.

Dan D. Rogers was a member of the university's Board of Trustees for thirty-seven years, serving on numerous building committees and on the Board Athletic Committee. An annual award, the Dan D. Rogers Ring, is still given for a football team member chosen as the most valuable player.

The memory of this TCU graduate, who was a respected leader in the church, business, and civic communities of Dallas, inspired the fund-raising campaign to build the hall that would honor his name. Dan D. Rogers Hall was completed in the summer of 1957 at a cost of $825,000, most of which came from contributions of Dallas businessmen and industrialists who were colleagues and friends of Rogers.

Although a graduate of Texas A&M, M. J. Neeley showed an early interest in TCU after he and his wife, Alice, established residence in the Park Hill section of Fort Worth near the campus. From an early business success developing Hobbs Manufacturing Company in Fort Worth, Neeley became a leader in other successful ventures in banking and industry.

In 1947, Neeley was elected to the university's Board of Trustees, thereby entering upon an extremely active tenure that lasted twenty-five years. In that time, he served on many committees that set policy and determined direction for the school and was directly involved in the fund-raising, planning, and construction of no less than seven major build-

54

ings, including the one which first housed the M. J. Neeley School of Business, Rogers Hall. In 1972, he retired as Chairman of the Board but continues as an honorary trustee well into his tenth decade of life. In recognition of this extraordinary man's personal service and his generous financial contributions, the school in 1967 bestowed upon him the honorary Doctor of Letters.

The name of Tandy is known throughout the world as a leader in the electronics and computer industries. After graduation from TCU in 1940, a year at Harvard Business School and a brief stint in the Navy, Charles David Tandy set about acquiring the

Charles David Tandy (courtesy Mary Couts Burnett Library).

Tandy Hall, about 1989 (courtesy University Publications).

small businesses that would eventually grow into the giant Tandy Corporation. He first started a chain of successful leathercraft stores throughout the United States. Then, in 1963, Tandy negotiated acquisition of a Boston electronics firm, Radio Shack Corporation, which would become internationally known with annual profits estimated at $2 billion. When Tandy died in 1978, an endowment from his estate and that of his widow, Anne Burnett, established the Anne Burnett and Charles Tandy Foundation. A major gift from the foundation provided the funding necessary to begin planning TCU's new business facility. Outside the Tandy Hall board room to the north of the ground floor atrium is a bust of Charles Tandy. A full-length oil portrait of the entrepreneur hangs just inside the reception area of the Charles Tandy American Enterprise Center on the third floor. A business chair, the David L. Tandy Executive-in-Residence, is named in honor of Charles Tandy's father.

LOWDEN AND PRINCETON STREETS

IF mood and weather permit, a short side trip is recommended that will take you along a quiet street or two of the residential neighborhoods bordering campus land. If you decline this option, exit the west entrance of Tandy Hall and follow the mall walk toward the large building next on your right, the Mary Couts Burnett Library.

Those opting for the alternate route will exit the east door of Rogers Hall and turn north toward Lowden Street. Lowden and Princeton streets, along with other streets north and east of the campus, were part of residential property developed soon after the school opened in Fort Worth in 1910. By the 1920s, most of the homes that lined these streets were occupied by faculty and staff of TCU. Beginning in 1924, the university began to purchase the land and houses and now owns all but a small portion of the blocks bounded on the south and north by Lowden and Cantey streets and on the west and east by University Drive and Parmer Street.

Several of the former homes in this section house university programs. Quartered at 2800 West Lowden, in the two-story brick and frame house, is the Department of Aerospace Studies and the Air Force ROTC. Continuing north on Parmer, then west on Princeton to the southwest corner of Greene, the walk leads to Alumni House, an attractive gray-painted brick home in which the Alumni Association offices are located. Two brick houses west on Princeton from the Alumni House provide office space for the Campus Police and for Personnel Services. Across the street is a brick apartment building dating from 1928. Owned by TCU and used as rental property, it is listed in the recent Tarrant County Historic Resources Survey as an intact example of Mediterranean-style architecture. On campus it is sometimes called "the castle" because of its architecture.

Turn south now on Greene back toward Lowden Street, where four more former residences have been converted to serve university needs. On the northeast corner of Greene and Lowden, a one-story frame structure houses Pastoral Care, while next to it a part of the campus maintenance department occupies a small brick home. On the northwest side of Lowden are two frame houses, formerly faculty residences, that date from the 1920s. The two-story corner house is used by Facilities Services and in the smaller house farther west are the offices of the TCU Press. Inevitable institutional expansion threatens the continuing existence of all of these places.

Mary Couts Burnett Library, about 1928 (author's collection).

MARY COUTS BURNETT LIBRARY

O<small>N</small> the morning after the devastating fire in Waco that destroyed the main building and the school's library housed within, Librarian Nell Andrew held aloft the *Waco Semi-Weekly Tribune* that had just been delivered and exclaimed: "With this paper we shall begin the rebuilding of the T.C.U. Library." Instead of Waco, of course, the rebuilding would take place in Fort Worth.

Mary Couts Burnett Library, about 1959 (courtesy
University Publications).

From 1911 until 1925, the library was provided
space on the second floor of the Administration
Building (now Reed Hall) in a main reading room just
twenty-four by thirty-six feet and a stack area of the
same dimensions just below on the first or
"basement" level. Increased acquisitions and student
enrollment soon led to a need for additional space. In
1923, when the need seemed most critical, TCU became the recipient of a gift that would undergird the
school's financial foundation for years to come — the
Mary Couts Burnett Trust. A stipulation of the bequest was that $150,000 be set aside immediately for

the construction of a building and, at the suggestion of then-President E. M. Waits, the building to be erected was the Mary Couts Burnett Library.

The library was the first building to be located on university property bordering the east side of University Drive. Prior to the library's construction in 1925, this undeveloped hardscrabble land had been used primarily as an athletic field. The small football stadium, Clark Field, a cinder track, and a baseball diamond were located there. The rest of the land was covered with the ever-present Johnson grass and a few wildflowers among which scudded the little "horned frog." After the football field was relocated in 1930 and until the Winton-Scott Hall of Science was built in 1952, the library stood solitary on this side of the campus.

Little remains to view of the exterior of the initial library building, for two subsequent enlargements, one in 1958 and the other in 1982, surrounded and subsumed the original building and grounds. But the camera recorded the changes in style and aspect from then to now, and memory recalls a landscaped sunken garden with its graceful pool of goldfish gliding in the shade of lily pads.

As you face the flight of steps that provide approach to the south-facing entrance of the library, an interesting view of the architectural styles to which the building has played host is provided. The three phases of construction that began in 1925 and that have led to the library as we know it today are evident primarily in the windows of this southern aspect. The tall, multi-paned ones of 1925 — the arched shape of which forms the logo of the library — give way on the west to the rectangular look of the 1958 addition and on the east to the glass walls and sharper angles of the 1982 addition. To the latest architect's credit, however, 1925 seems comfortably sandwiched between and is compatible with 1958 and 1982.

The design of the original Mary Couts Burnett Library was that of the local architectural firm of W. G. Clarkson and Company. The 1958 expansion was constructed according to the plans drawn by Joseph R. Pelich, Hedrick and Stanley, and Preston M. Geren, Associated Architects. Renowned architect Walter Netsch of Skidmore, Owings and Merrill of Chicago was the designer of the 1982 addition.

The story of the library's namesake, Mary Couts Burnett, is at once tragic, poignant, and heroic. Born in 1856, Mary Couts was one of five daughters of Colonel James Robertson Couts, prominent banker and rancher of Parker County. Her father was an admirer of Addison Clark and had made gifts to the pioneer institution during the Thorp Spring days. Mary Couts became the second wife of S. Burk Burnett, a wealthy Fort Worth cattleman. The one child born to the couple, S. Burk Burnett, Jr., died as a young man.

By 1920, the relationship between husband and wife had grown tense and Mrs. Burnett began to express fears that her husband was trying to kill her. Burnett claimed in court that his wife was suffering from "hallucinations" and won a sanity judgment against her. He was then successful in having her committed to limited asylum in a private Weatherford home, where she was kept virtually a prisoner until she engineered her own release on the very day, in 1923, of Burk Burnett's death. With the good counsel of her physician, Dr. Charles Harris (who later founded the Harris College of Nursing), she set about to free herself from the charge of insanity. She would also have to fight, in court, for her "widow's half" of the Burnett estate, which her husband had willed almost entirely to his granddaughter by an earlier marriage, Anne Burnett (later Tandy).

Not long after having won the battle for the Burnett estate, seemingly "out of the blue" she made her bequest to the university of over $3 million in trust. This was in December of 1923. Before that

61

time, Mrs. Burnett had shown no apparent interest in either the school or, indeed, the world of academe, and one story has it that her husband had quite pointedly indicated that none of his money would ever go to a religious concern nor to an institution of higher learning. The story continues that it was knowledge of this that led Mary Couts Burnett, left without heirs, to make the bequest. Her choice of TCU as the recipient of her estate was purportedly guided by her physician, Dr. Harris, and perhaps by recollection of her father's support of AddRan College.

By the fall of 1924, the library building was well underway, but Mrs. Burnett was not to see it in its final splendor. She died just before its completion in December of that year. It is told, however, that prior to her death she was driven by the building in its finishing stages and was able to see and perhaps derive pleasure from the all-but-complete structure that would bear her name. The only known portrait of Mary Couts Burnett hangs on a wall just inside the reference room of the library.

Inside the contrasts and complements continue, moving from early to late and back again. In the lobby, for example, modern skylights form crisp triangular patterns of blue and purplish hues, while ghosts of earlier windows, their once-eastern gaze blinded now by the painted brick that forms the lobby's west wall, give silent testimony to the past. The modern reference room to the east contrasts with the Cecil and Ida Green Reading Room to the west. The Green Room was the reference room and the only public reading area in 1925, and the sturdy oak tables and chairs date from that time.

If ghosts there be on the campus, one would surely seek here in the old reading room for them. No other campus spot is remembered as long and as well as this grand room that has been witness to such a range of human activity from serious study to gala

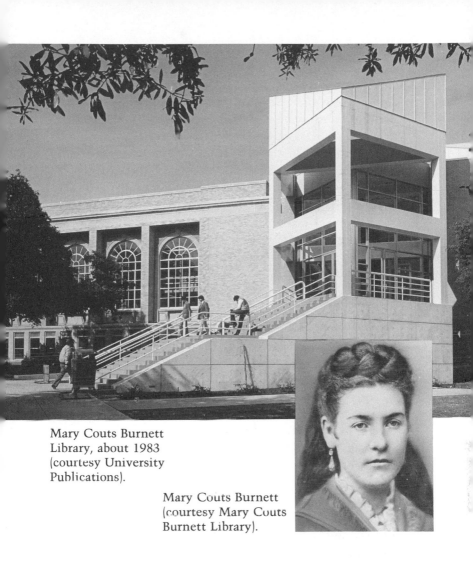

Mary Couts Burnett
Library, about 1983
(courtesy University
Publications).

Mary Couts Burnett
(courtesy Mary Couts
Burnett Library).

receptions to budding college romances. As a librarian currently on the staff I attribute my choice of
profession to the fact that my parents, Professor of
Biology Willis Hewatt and Elizabeth Harris, were
wed here in a ceremony conducted by the college
president. Music was provided by a faculty ensemble,
and the reception was prepared by the college cafeteria staff, headed by the bride's mother, Mrs. Georgia
Harris.

63

From its modest beginnings on the Fort Worth campus, the Mary Couts Burnett Library's collection has grown to over one million items, most of which are housed in open stacks. A state-of-the-art computerized system provides access to the materials in this depository of knowledge. Among its special collections are the papers and office paraphernalia of former Speaker of the United States House of Representatives Jim Wright. A replica of his Washington office and collection exhibits are located on the second floor east. In addition, the library is repository for the archival records and audio- and videotapes of the Van Cliburn International Piano Competitions, the American Hymnal Society holdings, and the William Luther Lewis Collection. This last contains works, many of which are first editions, of eighteenth- and nineteenth-century English and American writers. Premier in the collection is one of only two copies known to exist of the complete edition of nine quartos of Shakespeare printed by Thomas Pavier in 1619.

Another recent acquisition, an especially fine reproduction of *The Book of Kells*, is on view to the public inside the offices of Special Collections on the second floor. The volume was a gift of Mrs. W. A. Moncrief, a member of a family whose community and institutional support continues to be generous.

Leaving the library, retrace your way down the front entrance steps and follow the pavement west, turning right at the first intersecting walk toward the religion center located in buildings immediately north of the library. On the way you may want to stop and rest in the shaded pleasance that lies just between the far west end of Lowden Street and University Drive. This small park area, landscaped in 1987, was a gift of the TCU House of Student Representatives in honor of Mary Evans Beasley, wife of the late Theodore P. Beasley. The Beasleys generously supported numerous programs on the campus throughout many years. The commemorative stone in the garden simply, but eloquently, says of Mary Evans Beasley that she is "a friend of students."

RELIGION CENTER

In 1953 in a significant departure from tradition, architect Joseph R. Pelich designed the religion center complex along Georgian Colonial Revival lines, the single instance of this style on the campus. Tradition and traditionalists were further outraged by the selection of the masonry color. TCU President Sadler, weary of being asked why the new buildings were "red" rather than the usual buff, said: "In the first place they are not red, they're pink. The architects felt that this shade of brick would harmonize with the other buildings, and would be more appropriate for a chapel." Viewing the religion center now with its centerpiece, the Robert G. Carr Chapel, and trying to imagine it cream-toned and red-roofed, one would have to agree that the choice of style and brick was just right.

Preliminary plans to relocate Brite College of the Bible from what is now the Bailey Building had called for a dual-purpose unit. One section would house the graduate studies of Brite and the other would accommodate undergraduate religion studies, as well as provide classroom space for other AddRan College courses. A large contribution and promise for complete funding from San Angelo rancher and oil man, Robert G. Carr, made it possible to add the beautiful chapel. Today the complex consists of the central chapel, a south wing that houses Brite Divinity School, and a north wing, Beasley Hall, that provides offices and classrooms for the Department of

Robert Carr Chapel and the Brite Divinity School wing of the Religion Center, about 1986 (courtesy University Publications).

Religion Studies. An enclosed cloister along the back of the chapel joins the three units.

The two identical three-story wings contain primarily classrooms and offices. On the basement level in the Brite building is a large community room with a kitchen. Weatherly Hall was named in honor of John F. Weatherly, whose family provided funds for the hall; a portrait of Weatherly can be viewed within. In recognition of their support, the university conferred an honorary degree on Mrs. Maggie Weatherly, a member of the family and leading churchwoman of Panhandle, Texas.

Completed in 1954, Robert Carr Chapel, with its

Lucas C. Brite (courtesy Mary Couts Burnett Library).

Edward "Eddie" McMinn Brite (courtesy Mary Couts Burnett Library).

137-foot spire, has become a TCU landmark and can be seen from high-rise windows in downtown Fort Worth. The chapel incorporates a number of design elements from American Colonial churches, recommended by the wife of the president, Mrs. Frances Sadler, who travelled throughout the eastern states studying both architectural and decorative styles. The results of her research and the high quality of her taste are reflected in the simple elegance of Carr Chapel.

Ionic stone columns support the pedimented entrance portico; cornices here and elsewhere around the walls are underscored with deep dentils. The spire is an exact replica of the one atop the famous Old Lyme Church in Connecticut, and the appointments in the chapel interior continue the replication of early American structures. The brass chandeliers are after the design of those in St. Michael's Church in Charleston, South Carolina; the pulpit is patterned

Robert G. Carr (courtesy
Chancellor's Office).

Theodore Prentiss Beasley
(courtesy University
Publications).

after those in King's Chapel of Boston and Christ
Church in Cambridge. The arched heads of the Palla-
dian windows that grace both the chapel and the
cloister walls reflect the style of Mount Vernon and a
church in Watertown, Massachusetts. Dark mahog-
any, white, and deep scarlet enhance the interior
simplicity of this quiet place of worship.

The present organ in Carr Chapel was built by the
Ross King Organ Company of Fort Worth. It replaced,
in 1979, the original two-keyboard, fourteen-stop Reu-
ter organ. The King, valued at $295,000, has three
keyboards and thirty-six stops. The chapel carillon,
built by the Cincinnati firm of Verdin, was installed
in 1984, replacing an earlier one provided by Robert
Carr.

The carillon is electronic, not, as one would ex-
pect, a cast-bell mechanism. Through an architectural omission, the chapel tower will not accommodate the hoisting of bells, and architectural design

further prohibits renovation for tower bells. But the Verdin carillon that plays the short measures of the TCU alma mater before striking each hour is a close approximation to cast bells and the tonality is clean and clear.

The chapel is in constant use for student worship services, campus memorial services, and as a classroom for student preachers. It is also heavily booked throughout the year for wedding ceremonies.

The land on which the religion center stands was bought in the early 1920s from landowners Robert L. Green and John L. Cassell. Until sometime in the 1930s, Lowden Street was named Cassell Boulevard. Several large homes which stood on the property were converted to residences for women when Jarvis Hall, the only campus provision for women, was at capacity. Still active memory fondly recalls warm relationships that had their genesis in the rooms of Sterling Cottage on Lowden, Reed Cottage on Princeton, and Gibson House, farther north, near the southwest corner of Cantey and University Drive. A two-story brick home on the northeast corner of Princeton, once owned by the Green family, was used by the university from around 1948 to 1975, first by the development office and then by the Speech and Hearing Clinic of the School of Fine Arts.

The history of the eighty-year-old divinity school parallels much of that of the university itself. From Thorp Spring days, the school continuously offered studies in the Bible, but it was not until 1895 that a charter was obtained for "The Bible Department." The first chair of that department, J. B. Sweeney, gave impetus to a plan that would establish and endow a "Bible Chair" and later a Bible College.

The precipitous event that secured the chair and the college for TCU is thought to be a baptism in 1897 near the small West Texas town of Marfa. Addison Clark, co-founder and then-president of the young school, had come by invitation to preach.

Among the listeners that day were wealthy cattle-man Luke Brite and his wife, Eddie, nee Edward McMinn Anderson. Inspired by the words of the Reverend Clark and by the thought of what the church could mean to themselves and to future generations, both husband and wife confessed publicly and were baptized the same day into the Disciples of Christ denomination. The Brites' story of the building of their western cattle kingdom, the hardships and tragedies they knew, their unshakable faith, and their steadfast generosity is told more fully in the book-length *Brites of Capote* by Noel Keith and in an article entitled "The Brite Legacy" by Jane Pattie.

Suffice it to say that when asked for his support in developing the divinity program at TCU, Lucas Charles Brite hesitated only long enough to "talk over [the] proposition with Mrs. Brite" and within two weeks thereafter the College of the Bible was assured of $25,000 to be used for a suitable building to house its program. In subsequent actions, the Brites donated $25,000 to endow a chair of English Bible and a total of $37,750 toward the Bible building. Over protest from the donors, the college was designated Brite College of the Bible. Brite was the second "college" within the university — AddRan was the first.

Mr. Brite was elected chairman of the Brite College Board of Trustees in 1926 and served in that capacity until 1941. On September 4 of that year, Brite died following an emergency appendectomy. Valedictories included these words from future governor Coke Stevenson: "Luke Brite was a great-hearted builder of enduring things that will preserve his memory forever in the hearts of Texans. He served the Church, the State, and his fellowmen with a sincerity that endeared him to all who knew him"; from R. E. Petross, friend to Brite and agent at Marfa for the Southern Pacific Railway, "He told me that his supreme purpose in life was to do good. We thank God that He blessed this man with the means to spread the gospel, relieve want, and contribute to the moral and spiritual uplift of thousands."

Mr. Brite was on the university Board of Trustees from 1912 until 1941 and on the Brite Board from 1914 to 1941. Mrs. Eddie Brite finished the unexpired term of her husband on the Board of Trustees of Brite College and the university Board as well, her tenure on both lasting up to her death in 1963.

If any one name may be said to have achieved legendary status in the history of Brite Divinity School, it is surely that of Colby D. Hall. Educated at Add-Ran, Transylvania, the College of the Bible, and Columbia University, Dr. Hall became dean of the Brite College in 1914 and served in the post for an astonishing thirty-three years. He also served as dean of the university from 1920 until 1943.

In 1963, the name of Brite College was changed to Brite Divinity School. It is one of six schools of TCU but the only one that is a separate corporation and that raises its own endowment money. Brite, now a graduate school, has been accredited by the American Association of Theological Schools since 1939 and is the largest Christian Church-Disciples of Christ seminary in the nation. Because of its relationship with TCU, Brite uses many of TCU's services and even shares its chancellor. The main library houses the Brite collection, although the Brite librarian is on the seminary's payroll.

Theodore P. Beasley, after whom the building housing the AddRan Department of Religious Studies is named, was appointed a member of the Board of Trustees in 1954 and was a major benefactor of the school. Beasley was nationally prominent in affairs of the Christian Church (Disciples of Christ) and was a business, civic, and religious leader in Dallas. He was recipient of many honors, among them the Lay Churchman of the Year award of the Religious Heritage of America, Inc. in 1952 and, in 1965, a citation

71

from the National Conference of Christians and
Jews. TCU conferred on him the honorary Doctor of
Laws degree in 1968.

MOUDY BUILDING

THE J. M. Moudy Building for Visual Arts and
Communication represents an even more radical
break with traditional TCU architecture than the
"pink" religion center. The extensive use of "raw"
concrete, off-white masonry, and glass caused a controversy then, and years later still has its advocates
and critics.

Designed specifically for academic studies in art,
journalism, radio-television-film, and speech communication, the two-part, $16 million structure was a
gift to the university from the Amon G. Carter Foundation, represented then by Amon G. Carter, Jr.,
Ruth Carter Johnson (now Stevenson), and Katrine
Deakins. Mrs. Johnson was responsible for choosing
the Connecticut architectural firm of Kevin Roche,
John Dinkeloo and Associates. The Moudy Building
was the first Texas project of these architects, who
were internationally noted for their "glass clad" de-
signs.

In the conceptual design of the building, Roche's
primary consideration was the already existing architectural environment and the site on the corner of
University Drive and Cantey Street. Roche explained
that his selection of plain uncolored brick related it
to other campus buildings, and he purposely set back
the south wing of Moudy so as to provide a view of
the columnar entrance to the Carr Chapel. Roche
was of the opinion that "what happens on that site
[the northernmost entrance to campus grounds], will
give one the first impression of what TCU is."

If you stand on the street curb squarely in front of

the Moudy Building and face west, you can see at
least a little of what TCU is and has been. You can
see the classical columns of the 1911 Jarvis Hall
clearly across University Drive to the left and the
Georgian front of the 1949 Landreth Hall directly
across the street. University Christian Church with
its 1930s Spanish-style architecture is catercorner to
the right across University Drive, and moving a
fourth-turn to your left, you can see through and
above the live oak branches to the colonial lines of
the religion center with its towering chapel spire.
Turning full round, you see close up the modern

J. M. Moudy Building for Visual Arts and Communication,
about 1990 (courtesy University Publications).

lines of the 1982 concrete-masonry-glass Moudy Building.

Entrance to both wings of the Moudy complex is through a three-story-high octagonal atrium under a protective canopy of tempered glass. The center of the atrium is open to the sky and is landscaped with magnolia trees and other native flora. Benches edge the wide walks near the periphery of the planted area. Intended as a "place where students, faculty, and visitors can sit and enjoy a few moments of rest," the atrium also attracts colonies of birds which inhabit the upper reaches of the canopy.

There has never been any doubt about the superb facilities within the Moudy Building. With the exception of the office of the Dean of the School of Fine Arts, the north wing is given over to the art department with its varied activities ranging from painting and commercial art to photography and ceramics. This section includes high-ceilinged studios with an abundance of north light, photography laboratories and darkrooms, huge kilns for firing all kinds of ceramics, a multi-media room, and a slide library. A gallery on the ground floor regularly displays faculty, student, and community art work. A 154-seat lecture hall serves the entire campus.

The south wing contains the radio/TV/film department on the first floor; the studios of the university-operated radio station, KTCU-FM, are visible from the atrium. The journalism department occupies the second floor, where the campus newspaper, *The Daily Skiff*, and the student quarterly magazine, *Image*, are electronically typeset. The journalism department has the only curriculum within Moudy that is not under the School of Fine Arts umbrella. It is an academic unit of the AddRan College of Arts and Sciences.

The third floor of the south wing houses the Division of Communication in Human Relations. The

James M. Moudy (courtesy Mary Couts Burnett Library).

Moudy Building's design emphasis on specialized spaces for specialized studies is, perhaps, nowhere more evident than here. Lecture rooms with lecterns equipped with audience feedback controls, a room with walls that can be converted from mirrored to solid at a touch, and other devices and settings likely to be encountered professionally are an integral part of the instructional environment.

Following the desire of the donors, the building was named in honor of James M. Moudy, chancellor of the university from 1965 to 1979. Prior to his appointment as chancellor, he had served as dean of the graduate school and as academic and executive vice chancellor. He was the first TCU alumnus to be named its chief executive; his successor and the current chancellor, William E. Tucker, is the second.

During Moudy's tenure, first as vice chancellor for academic affairs and then as chancellor, six research-oriented doctoral programs were established and the Honors Program begun. His emphasis on a strengthened academic program brought to TCU recognition of quality in the liberal arts and in the sciences. During his regime, also, chapters of Phi Beta Kappa and Sigma Xi were brought to the campus. In 1979, the year of Dr. Moudy's retirement, the school further recognized his devoted and able leadership by conferring the honorary Doctor of Laws. The building named in his honor was dedicated in 1982.

THREE

The West Campus

LANDRETH HALL

Built in 1949 at a cost of $1.5 million, what is now designated as Landreth Hall would claim several "firsts." It was the first classroom building to be added to the campus since 1914, when Brite College was constructed, and the first permanent structure to be used for instructional purposes since 1921 when the gymnasium was built. Initially calling for a domed structure with a decorative cupola atop, the plan was altered to the present style when it was evident funds would not be available for the more elaborate building. Even then it had to wait three years for full funding.

Completed, the building was the largest of its kind in Texas, if not in the South, and was the only structure in the nation providing complete teaching space and equipment for all the arts under one roof. In fact, additional space made it possible to add new programs, some of which would grow to become popular and productive units of the fine arts school. The Division of Ballet and Modern Dance and the radio/TV/film department are notable examples.

Since 1978, Landreth has been home solely to music performance and pedagogy curricula. The other units of the School of Fine Arts and Communication are housed in the Moudy Building, the Ballet Building, and the Miller Speech and Hearing Clinic.

The fine arts building was designed by the team of architects that had responsibility for the many buildings erected from 1949 through 1965 — Wyatt Hedrick, Preston Geren, and Joseph Pelich. The exterior style resembles the earlier columned campus buildings, but instead of prominent freestanding structural elements, the columns are engaged. In addition, the entrance façade with its steps mounting from each side reflects neo-Georgian architecture rather than the earlier classical look. Pelich later patterned the remodelling of Reed Hall in the same style, sans columns.

The exterior of Landreth is a bit more ornate than other campus buildings, using stone carvings liberally. Most are generic, having little or no symbolism, but one bears special notice. In the pediment over the outer entrance to the University Theatre is a particularly appealing rendition of ladies, clad in classical attire, engaged in terpsichore. The extensive use of the cast stone is given brief relief in the Tennessee Tavernelle rose marble panels to either side of the north and south entrances to the main hall.

The structure is actually composed of three main units. The auditorium that seats 1250 occupies a central position and extends up through the three floors above basement level. On each of these floors, the great hall is flanked on three sides by offices, studios, classrooms, and practice rooms. The University Theatre, with a seating capacity of 225, provides an intimate setting for campus drama. It lies along the west side of the building with an entrance on the north off Cantey Street. Dr. T. Smith McCorkle, dean of fine arts from 1942 to 1955, is given credit for planning and overseeing the construction of the inte-

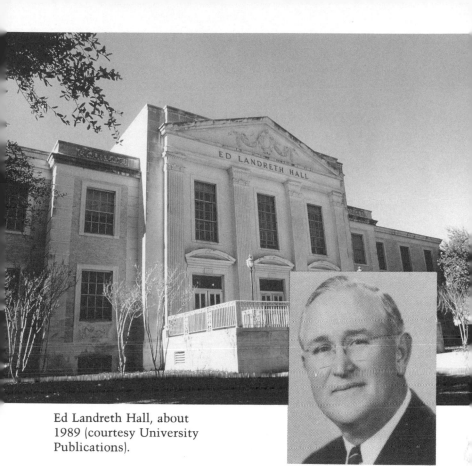

Ed Landreth Hall, about 1989 (courtesy University Publications).

E. A. Landreth (courtesy Mary Couts Burnett Library).

rior space of Landreth Hall. His portrait, along with that of Ed Landreth, is displayed in the foyer of the building.

Landreth Hall is probably the most internationally noted of the TCU campus buildings, for it has become known as the home of the quadrennial Van Cliburn International Piano Competition. All preliminary and semi-final sessions of the competition take place here. The acoustics in the main auditorium are especially fine, having been enhanced in 1973 from the original "dead" sound surface treatment. Following instructions from David Nibbilen, an acoustician from the Möller Company of Hagerstown, Maryland, the renovation included the addition of hard plaster and curved surfaces to provide enough reflective surface for good sound travel.

The auditorium also houses a concert pipe organ, one of the largest in the South. Built by the Möller Company, the four-keyboard organ contains a total of sixty stops and is valued at $492,000. In addition, Landreth Hall houses three smaller organs for teaching and practice, and sixty-five pianos, including two nine-foot concert Steinways and fourteen other grands.

E. A. "Ed" Landreth, for whom the building is named, was an active member of the TCU Board of Trustees from 1940 to 1960, when he was voted honorary life membership. In 1941, university leaders recognized the need to enlarge the physical plant and "thoroughly equip" the small but growing college. Plans for expansion were approved, and in the words of Dean Hall, "all that was lacking to get it started was the person to be the sparkplug for raising the money." Such a man was found in Ed Landreth, a Fort Worth oil man, "a Methodist, and one who had attained the reputation of being able to elicit money from Fort Worth citizens in large sums and leaving them happy about it." Mr. Landreth enthusiastically threw himself into the work and as a result of his efforts, the girls' dormitory Foster Hall was completed before the interruption of the war years. After World War II, he was co-chairman of an expansion that undertook to raise $5 million for new buildings on campus, of which the building bearing his name was the first. Initially, the auditorium in the fine arts building was named in his honor; later the whole building was designated Ed Landreth Hall. In 1947, the university granted the honorary doctorate to this energetic and devoted TCU advocate.

University Christian Church, 1991 (courtesy University
Christian Church).

UNIVERSITY CHRISTIAN
CHURCH

ANOTHER optional tour visit is suggested at
this point — to the University Christian Church
across Cantey Street on the opposite corner from
Landreth Hall. Although no longer officially bound to
the university, the church's history and that of TCU
are so closely associated and have been so influenced

by one another that it seems appropriate to include UCC at least as a walk on the periphery.

In actual fact, the two were born and grew up together. In the long-ago of 1873 at Thorp Spring, the infant Add-Ran College was "adopted and endorsed" by delegates of Christian Churches in Texas, and chapel services were a part of the student's daily routine. As the school grew, so grew the school's "church," so that by 1900, now situated in Waco, the college catalog proclaimed that "there is under the supervision and control of the University, an organized Christian Church, which worships in the Chapel every Lord's Day."

In 1911, after the school's final move to Fort Worth, an organized church and Sunday school were established by TCU students, faculty, and residents of the university area. Colby D. Hall, who played so many important roles in the university's administration, was the first pastor. At this time, the membership had no meeting place of its own; Sunday services were held in campus buildings. Finally, in 1933, a modest structure was built that, with considerable subsequent expansions, has been home to the congregation ever since.

The present grounds and buildings represent the second enlargement since the original church was built. With the exception of minor repairs and refurbishing, the eastern front and south and north aspects of the main sanctuary remain intact from that early construction.

In 1951, additions and alterations were made which included expansion of the sanctuary and construction of both an education wing and the Chapel of the Good Shepherd which extends east from the west wing and runs parallel to the sanctuary. The bell tower was added at this time also, although the bells were not installed until 1963. In 1965, a second remodeling began, more than doubling the seating capacity of the sanctuary, and another education wing, named in honor of Colby D. Hall, was constructed.

The plans of the original Spanish-style building were those of W. G. Clarkson, in consultation with A. F. Wickes. Clarkson also was responsible for the 1951 addition, in consultation with Charles Betts. Preston Geren designed the 1965 expansion.

The 1933 church was of pink colored brick with finely detailed cast stone trim and red tiled roof. The brick was later painted its pale buff to protect the brick surface and to match the TCU campus tones. The round stained-glass window over the baptistery, designed by TCU artist Judith Oelfke Smith, symbolizes the school founders' high ideal of "Christian education." The circle symbolizes eternal life, the Greek cross is Christ, the Bible is the source book, the torch stands for enlightenment, wisdom, and learning, and the source of all learning is represented by the hand of God. Judy Smith also designed and executed most of the stained-glass windows in the sanctuary and in the Chapel of the Good Shepherd and designed and carved the gold-leafed cross over the baptistery window.

WOMEN'S RESIDENCE HALLS

Four residence halls for women lie immediately west of Landreth Hall. In addition to Jarvis Hall, they provide non-sorority housing for over one thousand residents on the main campus. All are built on an E-plan, Foster and Waits being the smaller of the four, and all are almost identical in architectural style. Architects Wyatt Hedrick, Preston Geren, and Joseph Pelich, who had been retained by the university to participate in the expansion program that spanned the years from 1941 to 1958, designed all four dormitories.

Foster was the first built (1942) and its "vaguely Classical-Colonial-Revival style," as described by the Tarrant County Historical Survey, would become a model for most of the residence halls built on the campus since. Foster was the first TCU building to have the red-tiled hipped roof with a gabled portico over the central entrance, and of course, the "TCU brick" was used to harmonize with the rest of the campus. Directly north of and facing Foster, Waits Hall was erected in 1948. Colby Hall dormitory came in 1957, and finally Sherley in 1958.

Without perspective, the four dormitories seem an undistinguished matched set of red-topped, yellowish boxes. They stand unique, however, in time, and name, and in the memories of those young girls whose "away" homes they have been over the past fifty years.

Foster Hall was named as a memorial to R. Houston Foster, president of the university's Board of Trustees and chairman of the Building and Grounds Committee at the time of his death in 1941. He had been a Board member since 1932 and a trustee of Brite College of the Bible since 1926. It was Foster who, in 1933, authored the initial document that defined a tenure policy for the university. Foster was a 1904 graduate of TCU, a distinguished attorney, a Christian leader and lay teacher. He and his wife, Bess Coffman Foster, were both active in TCU affairs and in church stewardship in Fort Worth. In recognizing the strength of his leadership, President Emeritus E. M. Waits eulogized Foster at the building's dedication: "His untimely death was an irreparable loss to the university, and city, and the state. His devotion and loyalty and high chivalrous deeds are enshrined in this memorial, more lasting than bronze."

Waits Hall was named in honor of Edward McShane Waits, president of the university from 1916 to 1941. At the time of his appointment, he was pastor of the Magnolia Christian Church in Fort Worth and had been secretary of the TCU Board of Trustees for five years. During Waits' term of office, TCU was elected to membership in the Association of American Colleges and the Southern Association of Colleges and Secondary Schools. He led the school through the Depression years between 1929 and the mid-'30s, personally knocking on the doors of Fort Worth's business community to solicit desperately needed funds to keep the college going and to meet its faculty payroll. It was during his time, too, that the school's enrollment rose from 367 students to over two thousand, and faculty increased from twenty to over one hundred.

Described by all who knew him as a wise, kind, and gentle man, "Prexy," in the words of his colleague Dean Colby Hall, "was known for the beauty of his phraseology and the prolificity of his poetical quotation, but not for rushing to the termination of a speech." Students of his day will recall his slow eloquence and distinctive southern Kentucky pronunciation as he conducted mandatory three-times-a-week chapel in the old Ad Building's auditorium. Memorable, too, is his discussion of TCU's name. After extolling the greatness of Texas and the high purpose of a university, he explained that the middle word "Christian" gave dignity and meaning to the other two.

Prexy's alma mater, Transylvania University in Kentucky, granted him the honorary Doctor of Laws degree in 1923, as did TCU, followed in 1924 by Austin College in Sherman, Texas. A nearby street was named after him also. A portrait of this "friendly soul," painted by the Russian painter Stephen Silagy, hangs in the Waits parlor.

Colby, the third residence hall in this area, is named for the late long-time Dean Colby D. Hall. The dorm has come to be called by Dean Hall's first name because of the awkward repetition in the

R. Houston Foster (courtesy Mary Couts Burnett Library).

Colby Dick Hall (courtesy Mary Couts Burnett Library).

phrase, "Hall Hall." Colby Dick Hall — no other figure, with the possible exception of the founding brothers Clark, has cast such a long shadow on the history of TCU. For sixty-seven of his eighty-eight years, Dean Hall's life paralleled that of the university. In the introduction to Hall's historical account of the first seventy-five years of the university, then-President Sadler wrote: "to tell the story [of TCU] with insight, understanding, comprehensiveness, and real meaning, demand[s] a writer who has known, lived and loved Texas Christian University. . . . Those who read this volume should understand that in a very real sense they are reading the autobiography of the writer."

Colby Hall attended Add-Ran University in Waco from 1896 to 1899. After receiving his B.A. from Transylvania and his M.A. from Columbia, he returned to the Waco area and in 1906 was listed as

E. M. Waits Residence Hall, about 1987 (courtesy University Publications).

Edward McShane Waits (courtesy Mary Couts Burnett Library).

the educational secretary for Texas Christian University; three years later he was listed as the "minister of University Church" which met on the campus. When the university moved to Fort Worth in 1910, Mr. and Mrs. Hall, the former Beatrice Tomlinson, moved also with their daughter, Bita May, who is TCU professor emeritus of French, Spanish, and Italian. Holding faculty positions as professor of Latin and of English Bible, Hall was elected as the first Dean of Brite College of the Bible in 1915, a post in which he was to serve until 1947. In 1911, he also accepted the role as the first pastor of a small campus congregation that would grow into the University Christian Church.

In 1920, realizing his particular leadership qualities, the school asked Hall to step into the recently vacated position of dean of the university. This he did in addition to retaining the deanship of Brite, and his influence as second officer of the university would extend over the next twenty-one years. In 1941, upon the resignation of President Waits, the Board of Trustees considered Dean Hall the likely successor to the presidency. He declined, however, regarding his age as a precluding factor. In 1943, he asked to be relieved as dean of the university but stayed four more years at the Brite College helm.

After retirement from his administrative duties, Dean Hall continued to teach courses in English Bible until 1950. He also served as president of the Texas Christian Missionary Society (1948 – 1953) and the Texas Convention of Christian Churches (1950 – 1951). Texas Christian University, the school he "lived and loved," acknowledged its indebtedness to this universally esteemed man with the bestowal of an honorary Doctor of Divinity degree in 1951.

While construction was in progress on the fourth of the women's dormitories, the trustees decreed that it be named Sherley Hall in honor of Andrew Sherley and the members of "a large family, all of whom have been and are active friends and supporters of the school." Spelling the name variously as Sherley and Shirley, the men and women of this early northeast Texas family have long been identified with TCU.

T. E. Shirley, an uncle of Andrew, was the first of the family involved in the school's affairs. A railroad man from Melissa, Texas, T. E. served on the TCU Board of Trustees from 1893 to 1917, being elected

Sherley Residence Hall,
about 1960 (courtesy
University Publications).

Andrew Sherley (courtesy
Mary Couts Burnett
Library).

T. E. Shirley (courtesy Mary
Couts Burnett Library).

W. M. "Bill" Sherley
(courtesy Sports Information
Office).

chair from 1899 through 1909. Called by Colby D. Hall "a man of spirit indomitable" and "financial savior," Shirley propelled TCU through the "seven lean years" in Waco (1895 – 1902) by taking a leave of absence from the H&TC railroad to devote his time to the job of raising money to discharge the school's indebtedness. He was, in fact, the first to contribute to the campaign with the then-great sum of $1000. It was also as a result of his solicitation that the first designated dormitory for women was built on the Waco campus in 1902.

Andrew Sherley served on the Board of Trustees from 1920 to 1945 and on the Brite College Board from 1921 to 1945. He, as his relative before him, was a tower of financial and moral strength during more of the university's lean years in the '20s and '30s. Finding himself in financial difficulties during the Depression, he made good on an earlier pledge of $100,000 by deeding to TCU a number of farms in Grayson and Collin counties, with the provision that Brite College share in the funds.

A son of Andrew, W. M. "Bill" Sherley continued the family's interest in TCU, serving as a Board member from 1949 to 1965, when he was given honorary status. He was most active as chairman of the Board Athletic Committee and was instrumental in pushing forward the building of the Daniel-Meyer Coliseum.

Yet another member of the Sherley clan was a faculty member for forty-four years, from 1927 until 1971. Miss Lorraine Sherley was feared and revered by English students who had the privilege of attending her lectures in Interrelation of the Arts and her courses in Shakespearean drama and the Age of Shakespeare. Miss Sherley was an early and steady contributor to TCU programs, and a significant part of her estate was left to her alma mater upon her death in 1984. An additional endowment established a chair for the Lorraine Sherley Professor of Literature.

Robert M. "Billy Bob" Sherley and his wife, Syd, currently maintain the family's support of TCU.

MILLER CLINIC

As you leave the dormitory area to continue the tour west toward Stadium Drive, take the walk that leads behind Sherley Hall and borders Cantey Street. The church directly across Cantey Street from Sherley dorm is University Baptist which, like University Christian, has no official affiliation with TCU, although it serves a significant campus membership. The brick schoolhouse immediately west of the church was formerly Alice E. Carlson Elementary School. Built in 1926, it was the first public school in the TCU area, and many a faculty child was taught within its walls. W. G. Clarkson, the same architect who designed the original Mary Couts Burnett Library and University Christian Church, was responsible for Carlson's Spanish Colonial Revival style. In 1991, the school housed a gifted students' institute, archives, and offices but has no connection with the educational programs at the university.

Situated at the southeast corner of the intersection of Cantey Street and Stadium Drive is TCU's Miller Speech-Hearing Clinic. A recessed drive marks the entrance off Cantey to the more than 11,000-square-foot building which was designed by Albert Komatsu and dedicated in 1976. A facility of the speech-communication department, the clinic houses undergraduate and graduate programs in speech-language pathology and habilitation of the deaf. In addition, the department offers a program in bilingual communica-

sessions. Peripheral to this central section are classrooms for adults and children, evaluation rooms, two audiological testing suites, a "science" laboratory, faculty offices, and a conference room. This last is dedicated to the memory of Frank C. Hughes, dean of the School of Fine Arts from 1960 until his death in 1973.

Miller Clinic is a bright and cheerful place, with primary blues, reds, greens, and yellows predominating. Special equipment is everywhere in evidence, ready for a special staff to use in testing, evaluating, and teaching.

STARPOINT SCHOOL

IMMEDIATELY north of the Miller Clinic and facing Stadium Drive is another Komatsu-designed structure with the bright name of Starpoint School. Here, exceptional children learn in exceptional ways.

The life-size bronze in front of the low, modest building is the only piece of outdoor sculpture on the campus that is specific to the purpose of a building. Indeed, the Starpoint sculpture is the finial atop the light that shines from this place especially designated for the learning disabled. The statuary was commissioned in 1990 by M. J. Neeley in honor of his family and particularly to honor his wife, Alice Snead Neeley, who was instrumental in bringing Starpoint to the TCU campus. Based on a photograph of Mrs. Neeley's mother, Mary Brazelton Snead, and the two Neeley daughters, Marian and Kathleen, the work is entitled "Yearning to Know." It was sculpted by artist Randolph Johnston to depict the eternal bond of love and the spirit of teaching and learning. In dedicating the statue to the memory of his late wife, M. J. Neeley asked, "What greater thing could I do to recognize her love and her love for the family?"

Bronze statue, "Yearning to Know," in front of Starpoint School, 1991 (author's collection).

Alice and M. J. Neeley (courtesy University Publications).

The story of TCU's Starpoint is one of thoughtful caring and generous giving. It was the son of the Neeleys' daughter, Marian Nettles, who inspired the unique program. Russ Nettles had a learning problem for which his family sought help. They finally found the help he needed in New York City at a school directed by Mrs. Marguerite Slater, a pioneer in understanding learning disabilities and devising programs to counteract them. The New York school was named Star Point. The Neeleys, determined to help other children with similar problems, brought Mrs. Slater to TCU in 1966 to be principal of a new university-based school that would carry the same name. Mrs. Slater was succeeded after five years by her assistant, Laura Lee Crane, who retired in 1990.

Coordinated with the School of Education, the state-accredited Starpoint is owned and operated by TCU as a school for elementary-age children with diagnosed learning disabilities. It also serves as a training site for teachers and prospective teachers of children with perceptual handicaps.

The first Starpoint classes at TCU were held in the old Speech and Hearing Clinic in the "Green" house on Princeton Street, and after that in a wooden barracks building on the east campus — the same that now houses the Counseling Center. With the Neeleys' continued support and the financial contributions of a host of others, the permanent facility was completed in 1978. Other benefactors included Mr. and Mrs. George T. Abell, Mrs. O. C. Armstrong, Mr. and Mrs. Mark B. Clifford, Mr. and Mrs. Gene E. Engleman, Mr. and Mrs. Ben Fortson, Mr. and Mrs. W. R. Gibson, William A. Hudson and estate of Edwin R. Hudson, and Mr. and Mrs. F. Howard Walsh, as well as the Davidson Family Charitable Foundation, the Hoblitzelle Foundation, and the J. E. and L. E. Mabee Foundation.

The exterior style and use of material is in keeping with TCU architecture; the one-story flat-roofed aspect belies the space within. The interior is designed with the purpose of reducing distraction for the forty children who come here each year to learn. Central in the interior is a large open space with a staired pit for sitting, watching, listening, playing, and resting. School begins here with morning assembly. Four classrooms with workrooms and locker rooms are located north and south of the central space. Primary colors — red, blue, green, and yellow — predominate; each of the four classrooms use one of the colors as a theme. A gymnasium, kitchen and lunch room, library, and a classroom for the university's education students occupy the eastern portion of the building. Along the west front are the reception area, the director's office and a teachers' work area and lounge. Here are located portraits of the benevolent Neeleys and the innovative Marguerite Slater.

It is a peaceful place, this Starpoint, which invites special children to learn in special ways.

BROWN-LUPTON HEALTH CENTER

THE next three buildings on the walk have their names in common, all honoring in toto or in part the memory of Tom J. "Coca Cola" Brown. A member of the TCU Board of Trustees from 1940 to 1950, he was vice-president of the Fort Worth Coca-Cola Bottling Company. His great interest in TCU student life, especially that of the athlete, was made manifest in the construction of these buildings that bear his name.

In 1941, Brown made a pledge of $100,000, the largest commitment by any one individual to the building campaign initiated with the Sadler administration. Following World War II, he pledged another $300,000. Then, in partnership with his friend, Charles A. Lupton, he established the Brown-Lupton Foundation. A daughter of C. A. Lupton, Gloria Lupton Tennison, served on the TCU Board of Trustees at the time of her death in 1991.

The first of this trio of buildings encountered on the tour is the Brown-Lupton Health Center, built in 1963. Designed by Preston Geren, the one-story buff-

97

Brown-Lupton Health
Center, about 1980
(courtesy University
Publications).

Tom J. "Coca Cola" Brown
(courtesy Mary Couts
Burnett Library).

brick structure conforms to the predominant TCU
architectural style.

Some health service had always been offered to
TCU students, but not until after the health center
was built in 1963 was full medical care provided.
The first infirmary on the campus was established in
1942 and was located in the northeast corner of
Jarvis Hall until 1948, when it was moved to the first
floor east of Waits Hall. Under the general but usu-
ally absent direction of a physician, the facility was

staffed by professional nurses. In 1962, Sam P. Woodson, Jr., manager of the Brown-Lupton Foundation, presented a check to the university in the amount of $192,000 for the erection of a health center building.

Not until 1973, however, was a full-time physician hired as director of the center. Dr. John Sanford "Jack" Terrell, the only person to occupy this position, now has a staff of three fulltime physicians, six nurses, and other health professionals. Until 1991, the health center operated as an around-the-clock hospital. Lack of funds, however, forced it to out-patient-only status, which may mean that dormitories will again need to provide quarters for cases requiring isolation — for example, contraction of the chicken pox virus, which regularly appears each semester among the student population.

The professional staff handles an average of 17,000 patients a year, often a hundred in a day, and is a major source of information to students on venereal disease, AIDS, drugs and other health risks. All athletic health care comes under the jurisdiction and supervision of the health center, as well, whose primary concern is not "who gets on the field, but who gets well." A TCU physician is always present at athletic contests.

BROWN-LUPTON STUDENT CENTER

An on-campus place for students to congregate socially came late to TCU. In the early Fort Worth years when the unbroken land still stretched out into fields and valleys surrounding the TCU hill, day-long picnics and excursions to the Trinity River north and west of the campus were on every weekend agenda. Large groups would hike the several miles to and from favorite sites. Some still remember learning to swim in the Trinity back before there was a gym and a swimming pool. After social mores relaxed in the early '30s to allow dating and dancing, the students still found no adequate and convenient space to exercise their recently granted privileges. But TCU students, as students everywhere will, found places for social interaction. One of the most popular sites during the '30s and '40s was the drugstore at the corner of Bowie and University, the soda fountain of which was always bustling with the student population from across the street.

The first designated "student lounge" area on the campus was in the basement of the old Ad Building. Heralded in the *Skiff* as "a dream come true," this lounge was opened and "presented" to the student body in April 1948. The lounge had a seating capacity of sixty-five, a soda fountain that cost $1600, a cigarette machine that would "save many a long trip to the drugstore," and a coin-operated jukebox for dancing. It was to operate until 10:30 P.M., and a statement attributed to then-President Sadler made it clear that "privileges of the lounge will be shared by both sexes." The ladies, it seems, had come a long way from the closely guarded days of Ida Van Zandt Jarvis and Sadie Beckham.

Two years later, the large room that now serves as the Faculty Center was designed as a study lounge. Plans were then for the Ad Building facilities to be entirely given over to the student union.

Provision of more space was slow in coming, however, and student unrest over the matter grew. Finally, in 1952, Dr. Sadler announced that a "friend" of the university had significantly increased the possibility of securing funding for a new structure to accommodate all student activities. The friend was Glen Woodson who, as manager of the T. J. Brown and C. A. Lupton Foundation, brought the need to the attention of his directors. The planned structure was what is now known as the Brown-Lupton Stu-

Brown-Lupton Student
Center at night, with Frog
Fountain in the foregound,
1969 (courtesy University
Publications).

Charles A. Lupton
(Courtesy the *Fort Worth
Star-Telegram* Photograph
Collection, Special
Collections Division, The
University of Texas At
Arlington Libraries).

dent Center. Completed in 1955, the building under-
went significant renovation and expansion in 1967
and 1991, again with generous funding from the
Brown-Lupton Foundation.

The student center houses the main kitchen and
cafeteria, several smaller food service areas, the University Store, offices and meeting rooms for the Student House of Representatives, a large common
study-lounge area, study rooms, the chancellor's din-

ing room, and the ballroom with its seating capacity of more than seven hundred. In addition, a number of other rooms are available for university-related functions. The largest of these, the Woodson Room at the north end of the second floor, is named in honor of Glen Woodson, who was appointed to the TCU Board of Trustees in 1955. In 1991, a nephew, S. Pat Woodson, III, headed the Brown-Lupton Foundation Board of Trustees and was also a member of the TCU Board.

The center is the design of Preston Geren and bears the architectural stamp of the mid-century building era at TCU. Buff brick, cast stone, and polished granite recall the Winton-Scott Building and the original Dan D. Rogers Hall and foreshadow the similar styling of the Rickel Building erected some twenty years later.

The westward view from the student center was not always so tidy. Where now there is the grass lawn and a central fountain with the high-rising stadium and domed coliseum beyond, there were once maintenance shacks and sheds with dirt-road access through the wild and weedy field. Once a dairy occupied a portion of this space; its cows supplied milk to the school's boarding facility. The dairy ceased operation before 1930, the wooden maintenance buildings were removed by the late '40s, and Frog Fountain was placed in the middle of the quadrangle area in 1969, courtesy of Mr. and Mrs. H. H. Phillips of San Antonio.

The fountain, designed by Buck Winn, has four stylized lotus petals from which water cascades to the pool below. The lotus was chosen because of its historic symbolic association with education. The original fountain had horned frog images set in the surrounding rock work, but weather and vandalism eventually took their toll and none remain.

Milton Daniel (courtesy Mary Couts Burnett Library).

Milton Daniel Hall, about 1982 (courtesy University Publications).

MEN'S RESIDENCE HALLS

THE four buildings directly south and west of the Frog Fountain quadrangle were built as residence halls; three of them remain in that service.

Tom Brown Hall, completed by the fall of 1947, was the earliest of the three buildings named in honor of "Coca-Cola" Brown. An enthusiastic follower of TCU's athletic fortunes, Brown was informed of the new structure's name at a surprise ceremony during half time of the 1948 spring training football game. Coach Dutch Meyer and Athletic Director Howard Grubbs presented the bottling company executive with a plaque on which was mounted a picture of the $325,000 dorm, and Meyer read a letter which officially informed Brown of the decision. The letter praised Brown's "long time interest and loyal support" and further stated: "it is entirely fitting that your inspiring association with successive student groups should be projected into the future in the naming of this modern new boy's dormitory. Tom Brown Hall is a name that is a symbol of grateful recognition of the fine part you have taken in the ongoing of Texas Christian University." The dorm initially had three "non-communicating" sections and housed 130 men including varsity athletes, who lived in the west wing. This was, in fact, the first designated residence area for TCU athletes.

The building immediately south of Tom Brown and facing it across the green has an uncertain future. Pete Wright Dormitory was built in 1955 as a men's residence hall, and, although structural problems and lack of occupancy demand were evident as early as 1974, it served in this capacity until 1988. Closed now, with the exception of a small area which houses the main campus telephone switchboard, it stands as an ironic, hollow tribute to the large personality after whom it is named.

Loy Calvin Wright, "Mr. Pete" — letterman, alumnus, athletic director, treasurer of the university, business manager, trustee — was apparently a rare species with no known enemies. Tall, angular, calm and calming, Mr. Pete was associated with the university for over sixty-eight years.

At the age of twenty-one, Wright entered TCU's preparatory department in 1904, when the school was still in Waco, receiving his high school diploma there in 1906. He graduated from the university's baccalaureate program in 1910, having distinguished himself especially as a tackle on the early Frog football teams, and being elected team captain in 1907 and 1909.

L. C. "Pete" Wright
(courtesy Mary Couts
Burnett Library).

After graduating, he was in association with Dan Rogers in the Dallas banking business until 1922, when he accepted a call back to the campus, now in Fort Worth, as athletic director. In 1932, Mr. Pete relinquished the athletic position and was appointed business manager and treasurer. As such he wisely managed TCU's business affairs for twenty-three years, retiring in 1955. He was elected to the Board of Trustees in 1957 and served until his death in 1972. Shortly before Wright's death, Houston journalist Morris Frank observed that "Pete is a symbol of what's right in the world."

Mr. Pete's personal sacrifices to bolster the institution during financial crises were well-known, working one year without benefit of salary and, along with his president, E. M. Waits, "walking the streets to meet the TCU payroll." It was also known that the serious would-be student who was in need of funds to underwrite a college education was counseled to go see Mr. Pete or his cashier, "Bud" Dunagan, who would more often than not find the needed support. Frequently, it was furnished from Mr. Pete's personal resources.

Among other honors that Wright received were the dedication to him in 1955 of the annual, *The Horned*

Frog, the Valuable Alumnus Award in 1959, and induction in 1967 into the TCU Ex-Lettermen's Hall of Fame. In 1989, remembering his uncle's dedication and generosity, Robert Wright and his wife, Mary, endowed a $100,000 business scholarship in honor of L. C. "Pete" Wright.

Directly south of the Wright building across Wright Drive is the HVAC (Heating, Ventilation, and Air Conditioning) Control Center and the Maintenance Annex, which was a practice gym until Daniel-Meyer Coliseum was built in 1961. Adjacent to these structures is the small building that houses the ROTC rifle range.

The third dormitory for men in this area is Milton Daniel, located west across South Drive from Tom Brown Hall. Built according to the now familiar design of Joseph Pelich, it was completed in 1957, as was its near mirror image, Colby Hall residence for women, which faces it across the quadrangle. Both Milton Daniel and Colby initially housed the eight fraternities and eight sororities introduced to the campus for the first time in 1956. In 1973, after the Greek chapters had settled into new quarters on the Worth Hills campus, Milton Daniel became home to the male athletes, remaining thus until Moncrief Hall was opened in September 1988. Milton Daniel has double-occupancy accommodations for approximately 320 men.

Milton Enoch Daniel, for whom the hall is named, was a 1912 graduate of TCU and, much like his colleagues in that era, was a lifelong supporter of his alma mater. Dean Colby Hall in his *History of Texas Christian University* says of Daniel: "[He] was a McLennan County boy who followed TCU to Fort Worth [and] returned in 1916 with his law degree from UT to become a Professor in the TCU Law School, and Coach. . . . He made a most valuable contribution in personality, in character, and in sportsmanship, foreshadowing his later leadership as an outstanding citizen in Breckenridge, and as a trustee, well deserving the honor of the LL.D. degree conferred on him at the 1945 Commencement."

In his student days, Daniel captained the football team in 1911 and served as registrar in 1911 and 1912. He briefly returned to the school as football coach, director of athletics, and instructor in the short-lived law school in 1916, before entering the military and serving in World War I.

Milton Daniel, as his friend and fellow-student Pete Wright was to do, helped hundreds of deserving students finance their education. It was reported that Daniel kept "thousands of dollars on deposit" at the university to be used for this purpose.

Throughout Daniel's tenure on the Board of Trustees (1927 – 1958), his influence was felt in many programs, but he was especially supportive of building campaigns, athletics, and ranch management. He had served as Chairman of the Board for five years when he died in 1958, leaving to TCU a gift second in value only to that of Mary Couts Burnett. Earnings from the approximately $7 million estate were assigned to TCU for the general development of the university and with no specific designations as to their use.

Moncrief Hall, the newest building on campus and the eighteenth residence hall, was occupied for the 1988 fall semester while some finishing touches were still being made. Heralded as the new athletic dorm, the building, designed by Albert Komatsu, can house 224 men and women and was intended primarily for student athletes. Since the 1991 National Collegiate Athletic Association sanctions against "athletic dorms," however, Moncrief Hall's tenure as exclusive to athletes was brief.

The architectural plan of Moncrief is somewhat different than previously built dormitories in that its shape is roughly that of a squared "Z," and it is four stories high, rather than the conventional three. The two wings are separated by the crossbar of the "Z"; women occupy the east wing, men the west. Also in contrast to other residence halls on the campus, Moncrief has seven small lounges instead of one or two large ones. Three of these are furnished as study areas, four are TV/recreation rooms. One large room, the Bess N. Fish Lounge, is reserved for special occasions. Located on a fourth-floor corner, it has a sweeping view of the athletic complex to the west, and from its bay windows one can actually watch a baseball game in progress on the Frog diamond south of Daniel-Meyer Coliseum. This room, used primarily to entertain recruits to TCU's athletic programs, is named for a major contributor to the university and an honorary member of the Board of Trustees.

All residents' rooms are arranged as suites, two rooms for double occupancy adjoined by a shared bathroom. Also unique to Moncrief are the "trash" rooms, which are specifically designed for receiving trash collected from rooms and deposited by the residents themselves. There are also three kitchens for use by residents, two vending rooms, two laundry rooms, and a spacious apartment for a student residence assistant.

The vaulted glassed entrance that faces north and the first floor lobby with a long counter that appears to simulate a "check-in desk" actually give Moncrief Hall the atmosphere of a hotel rather than a traditional college dorm. Readily accessible elevators add to the illusion.

As the name of the hall would imply, the dormitory was financed primarily by the W. A. Moncrief and W. A. "Tex" Moncrief, Jr., families of Fort Worth. Moncrief Hall is a manifestation of the family's interest in TCU athletics. "Tex" Moncrief, the living member of the father-son team, confessed at the dedication ceremonies of the $5.6 million structure, that he was a "dyed-in-the-wool Horned Frog fan," showing his "purple pride" by finalizing his

W. A. "Tex" Moncrief and
Chancellor William E.
Tucker (courtesy University
Publications).

Moncrief Hall, about 1988 (courtesy University
Publications).

Mr. and Mrs. W. A.
Moncrief (courtesy
University Publications).

speech with a booming "Let's go Horned Froggies!"

The Moncriefs have been generous supporters of university programs for many years. Three academic chairs have been endowed: the W. A. Moncrief, Jr., Chair of Physics, the Charles B. Moncrief Chair of Geology, and the W. A. "Tex" Moncrief Founding Chair of Engineering. The geology chair was given in honor of "Tex" and Deborah Moncrief's son, Charlie, who was a member of the TCU Board of Trustees from 1984 to 1992.

RICKEL BUILDING

FROM the south exit of the lobby of Moncrief Hall, a few steps will take you to the west front of the Cyrus K. and Ann C. Rickel Building for Health, Physical Education, and Recreation. The Rickel Center, as it has come to be called, occupies land at the northeast corner of Stadium and Bellaire Drive North, the former site of TCU's intramural fields. Joseph R. Pelich Associates were responsible for the architectural plan of the 140,000-square-foot building completed for use by September 1972. "TCU brick" faces the lower portion of the building, while cast stone-clad pillars support overhanging crushed stone panels, protection for the walk that partially surrounds the center on three sides. The dark rose granite of the wide entrance veranda and the vertical entrance pillasters provide design relief and interest. Under the organizational management of the Office of Student Affairs' Department of Recreational Sports, the Rickel Center provides TCU students, faculty, staff, and alumni with programs and facilities for a wide range of physical activities. To get an idea of the variety and the quality of recreational sports offered here, one needs to tour the interior.

Cyrus K. and Ann C. Rickel Building for Health, Physical Education, and Recreation, about 1980 (courtesy University Publications).

Bronze plaque honoring Cyrus K. and Ann C. Rickel.

Many rooms are locked when not in use, so it is wise to ask for a guide upon entering.

Inside is a plethora of activity rooms, as well as classrooms and offices. The aquatics center, occupying the major portion of the south side of the entry level floor, includes two pools, an adjoining outdoor terrace, and "wet" classrooms. The swimming and diving pools both meet or exceed NCAA standards.

Amon G. Carter Foundation, Earl E. Combest, Bess N. Fish, the George and Mary Josephine Hamman Foundation, the Kresge Foundation, the J. E. and L. E. Mabee Foundation, and the United States Steel Foundation.

Amon G. Carter (courtesy University Publications).

Amon G. Carter Stadium, about 1989 (courtesy University Publications).

FOUR

The Athletic
Complex

AMON G. CARTER STADIUM

Iғ you began with Jarvis Hall on this walk, you
have now concluded the tour of the main campus. If
you are continuing the journey to visit the athletic
complex and the Worth Hills campus, you may want
to retrieve your car, for there is quite a bit of walking
left and the route includes a hill or two.

This second part of the tour begins with the Amon
G. Carter Stadium, a high-rising structure whose
flying "T" logo is clearly visible in the west from
almost any spot on the main campus. Football came
to TCU before the turn of the nineteenth century.
The then-Waco college fielded its first team against
Toby's Business College of Waco in 1896, a year before the school colors and mascot were chosen. Since
that time, the purple and white Fightin' Frogs' fortunes have waxed and waned. In the early years in
Fort Worth, the athletic teams played as a member of
the Texas Intercollegiate Athletic Association, be-
coming members of the current Southwest Conference in 1923. Often competing with a roster of only
sixteen to eighteen men chosen from a total enrollment of some one hundred and fifty, "little TCU"
began to make itself known in the region.

The first football arena that provided spectator seating was Clark Field on the east campus, where parking lots are now located behind the Mary Couts Burnett Library. Encouraged and inspired by a 1929 Southwest Conference championship under the direction of Coach Francis Schmidt, TCU began to plan a modern permanent home for its champions in a natural "bowl" of land on a recently purchased tract of seventy-five acres to the west of the main campus. This early stadium was the design of architect Wyatt C. Hedrick. As originally planned, east and west stands would have a seating capacity of 20,000. Only the west stand, however, was built initially. Constructed entirely of reinforced concrete, the present arcaded exterior and blocky end bays were part of the 1930 structure.

In this new home, the "Froggies" would make history. They played their first game in the new stadium, then unnamed, on October 1, 1930, soundly defeating a University of Arkansas club by a score of 40 to 0. In 1932, they again snared the Southwest Conference championship with a perfect record against all other conference schools. But the real glory days were yet to come. The legendary Leo R. "Dutch" Meyer became head coach in 1934 and steered the Frogs not only to national recognition but also to a coach's dream — the designation in 1938 of No. 1 in the nation. Passing was the name of the game in those years and two of the passers, Slingin' Sammy Baugh and little Davey O'Brien, are still regarded as gridiron heroes in the history of collegiate football.

The east stands and end zone seating, erected during 1947 and 1948, increased the stadium's seating capacity to 33,000. It was in this construction phase that the carved stone all-sports murals were placed above the arcaded east front. In 1956, a second deck was added to the west stands, dwarfing the 1930 structure and upping the seat count to the present

45,627. That year another TCU name was added to the football immortals, that of the great running back, Jim Swink.

The stadium was nameless until 1951, when the Board of Trustees voted officially to designate it the Amon G. Carter Stadium in honor of the *Fort Worth Star-Telegram's* publisher and entrepreneur.

Stories with Amon G. Carter as the central character are legion. He was, after all, "Mr. Fort Worth." Many of the most colorful tales have to do with his exuberant support of the TCU athletic programs, especially in the '20s, '30s, and '40s, when the Fightin' Frogs were riding high on victory in football, and the baseball team was no slouch. Some said that Carter never had time for anything but a winner, and that was the reason the Frogs were "his" team. Others said that TCU's good fortune was to be in Fort Worth *and* be a winner, and that was the reason he touted them. He made no bones about Fort Worth and West Texas being "his" and if the Frogs fell within those bounds, few could find fault with it.

Once he adopted the TCU Horned Frogs, Carter's flare for showmanship took over. He chartered trains to baseball and football games and was foremost among the fans, encouraging dancing in the aisles and leading the band in impromptu pep sessions. According to biographer Jerry Flemmons, Carter coined the phrase: "Give 'em hell, but do it in a good Christian spirit," going on to define "Christian spirit" as "Knock 'em down, pick 'em up, dust 'em off and ask 'em how they feel. If they can answer, knock 'em down again."

Carter's finest hour came when Davey O'Brien won the Heisman Trophy in 1938. He chartered a plane to transport Davey and an entourage of TCU officials and friends to New York for the award ceremony and arranged to have a Knickerbocker stagecoach with six white horses and thirty men of the Staten Island Sheriff's Horse Guard meet his party.

With Dutch Meyer and TCU President Waits inside the coach and Davey on the driver's seat beside him, Carter took the reins and drove down Wall Street, waving his big Shady Oaks Stetson hat and yelling "Hooray for Fort Worth, West Texas, and TCU!" One can only imagine the modest Davey's thoughts amid all that hoopla.

With all the moral and financial support that Amon Carter gave, one wonders why it took so long to give his name to the Frogs' battlefield. It was Amon Carter who led an effort in 1923 to find contributors to a $50,000 fund to help clear the university's indebtedness. It was Amon Carter who headed the fund-raising campaign to erect the football stadium for the school after the championship of 1929. In fact, almost single-handedly (some say heavy-handedly) he raised the $450,000 necessary for its construction, paid for the electric scoreboard himself, and was an active consultant on the stadium's design. It was probably no mistake that when the west stands had been completed, they ran up sixty-one rows, one more than SMU's Owenby Stadium in Dallas.

DANIEL-MEYER COLISEUM

A NEW coliseum for the TCU basketball program had been in the university's long-range building plans for at least fifteen years before funds were finally available to begin construction in 1961. For twelve of those years, Coach Byron "Buster" Brannon carried architects' plans on recruiting trips, promising prospects that if they signed with the Frogs, they would have a swanky new court on which to play. Although Brannon continued as head coach through the 1966 – 1967 season, only a few of his recruits would ever bounce a ball on the hard maple floor of the facility. And although Buster coached the Frogs to four Southwest Conference titles, he never won one in what was early called "Buster's House." That honor was left to his successors, Johnny Swaim and Jim Killingsworth.

When TCU moved from Waco to Fort Worth in 1910, the upstairs gymnasium of the First Baptist Church in the city was home court. In 1921, the "little gym" was built, which provided a campus court until 1926 when a larger facility, the wooden "big gym," was constructed. The popularity of the sport and the condition of the "barn," as the "big gym" had come to be called, forced the Frogs in the mid-'40s to seek another place to play.

In 1947, Fort Worth's City Council voted an improvement to the city's large-capacity Will Rogers Coliseum — a portable hardwood basketball floor that could be laid on the arena surface, thus providing space not only for the university's games but for high school contests, as well. The first game in Will Rogers, a mile north of the campus, was between Poly High and Paschal High, followed the same evening by the first conference game of 1947 between TCU and Texas A&M. The "barn" continued as a practice gym until it burned in 1953.

With so many events taking place in the versatile Will Rogers, it became increasingly difficult to schedule basketball. In the 1955 season, TCU and the high schools began playing in the newly built Public Schools Gymnasium located to the east of the Will Rogers complex. Then, finally in 1961, the Frogs came home to the spacious Daniel-Meyer and have stayed home ever since.

The May 3, 1946, *Skiff*, shows a picture of a planned "Field House" in the squared boxy style then common to basketball gyms. As it turned out, of course, the now common circular arena with a center playing court and domed roof was ultimately built. In 1959, a tentative sketch of that design was

published in *The Skiff*. Joseph Pelich was chosen as
the final architect, ground was broken in March
1961, and the building was completed in December
of that year at a cost of $1.4 million. The Amon
Carter Foundation was again a major contributor.

The Daniel-Meyer Coliseum is built on two levels.
The east entrance is at ground level and opens into a
wide concourse that completely encircles the court
and spectator area. Eighteen entrances off the concourse provide access to the armchair seating that is
divided in an equal number of rows above and below
the concourse level. Seating capacity is 7166. For
events other than basketball, 1200 chairs can be
comfortably placed on the covered playing surface.
Special convocations, conferences, and commencement exercises are commonly held here. Outer walls
of the gym are painted aluminum and brick, and the
roof is a synthetic material laid on structural steel.
Most athletic staff offices and the main ticket office
are housed in Daniel-Meyer.

In 1964, an Ex-Letterman's Club Room was added
on the east, its windows overlooking the south end
zone of Amon Carter Stadium. Tastefully furnished
in purple and white, the room is used primarily for
club meetings and for entertaining recruits. On display are trophies garnered by TCU athletes over the
years, Davey O'Brien's Heisman Trophy among
them. A 1970 expansion improved dressing rooms,
added new training rooms, and provided player access
to the stadium by means of a tunnel leading from the
coliseum's lower level dressing area.

Even before the building was completed, the Board
of Trustees named it the Daniel-Meyer Coliseum, in
honor of Milton E. Daniel and Leo R. "Dutch"
Meyer. This was the second posthumous honor for
Daniel: a men's dormitory had been named after him
in 1957. The "Dutchman," however, was still on the
staff to enjoy the distinction. He retired as athletic
director in 1963.

L. R. "Dutch" Meyer (courtesy Mary Couts Burnett Library).

Daniel-Meyer Coliseum, about 1985 (courtesy University Publications).

Meyer's association with TCU began when he was a public-school student in Waco and a water boy for the TCU football team on which Milton Daniel played. Their association continued when Dutch entered TCU in 1917, the one year that Daniel was the Frogs' football coach. As a student athlete at TCU, Meyer lettered in three sports — football, basketball, and baseball. After graduation in 1922, he was basketball coach at Polytechnic High School in Fort Worth for one year, returning to TCU in 1923 as coach of freshman football, basketball, and baseball. Coaching varsity baseball in 1933, he saw his team win TCU's first Southwest Conference championship. From 1934 through 1952, he was head football coach, his teams winning three Southwest Conference championships, a national championship, and seven bowl game bids.

Dutch was one of those for whom the phrase "they broke the mold" surely was coined. He was a tough and fierce competitor and, as he was often heard to state, he didn't "like good losers." Whatever the contest, he meant to win, whether it was dominoes, bridge, fishing, baseball, or football. Every game was a battle — "put on your bonnets, boys, we're going to war" — and giving up was not allowed — "Fight 'em till Hell freezes over, then fight 'em on the ice!" Even while he was still an undergraduate he had acquired the nickname of "Iron" and a later version that stuck, "Old Ironpants."

With the exception of one year, Dutch's entire adult life was spent in some phase of athletics at TCU. Highly regarded and well-liked, the hard-nosed Dutchman maintained a genuine camaraderie with TCU administration and faculty, and especially with his long-time friends, "Mr. Pete" Wright and Milton Daniel. No one can question the appropriateness of the tribute implied in the naming of Daniel-Meyer Coliseum.

In addition to the two major structures, the athletic complex includes a track and baseball diamond and spacious public parking. The track lies on the hill directly west of the coliseum and the baseball diamond is directly south. Playing courts for the athletic tennis program and fields for non-athletic sports are located on the Worth Hills campus, which is south across Bellaire Drive North from the main athletic facilities.

AMES OBSERVATORY

SOUTH of Daniel-Meyer, up the Stadium Drive hill toward the Worth Hills campus, is the little

Ames Observatory, 1962 (courtesy University Publications).

Ames Observatory situated west of the intersection of Bellaire Drive North and Stadium Drive. As early as 1948, the idea of an observatory on campus was being considered. At that time, Miss Charlie M. Noble, a TCU instructor of anatomy, was an enthusiastic supporter of the idea. The large planetarium at Fort Worth Museum of Science and History is named for her.

In 1956, *Fort Worth* magazine published an article proposing an "astronomical center" for the campus. The center was to include a twelve-inch catadioptric telescope, other smaller telescopes, a spectroheliograph, a planetarium, laboratories, and classrooms. That plan was never realized, but a 1961 gift from C. B. Ames, then director of Fish Engineering Corporation of Houston and father of TCU student Dick Ames, did make possible the smaller observatory and a large part of its equipment. Outfitted with a twelve-inch telescope, the Ames Observatory is used by the Department of Physics as a laboratory for astronomy classes.

FIVE

Worth Hills

RESIDENTIAL AREA

THE university acquired the 106 acres of land comprising the Worth Hills campus in 1961. For thirty-eight years a municipal golf course, it was lo cally dubbed "Goat Hills" because of its rough and rolling topography. TCU's proposal to the Fort Worth City Council to buy the property set off a spirited debate among the citizenry, with primary opposition coming from the TCU-Westcliff Homeowner's League, many members of which owned homes bordering the course. In a city-wide election, however, TCU won the right to purchase Worth Hills, thereby gaining much-needed ground for future expansion. With money from the sale, the city built a new municipal course near Benbrook Lake to appease the naysayers.

The Worth Hills area of the campus is often called Greek Hill now, because five of the seven residence halls located there house TCU's social fraternities and sororities. Although initially opposed by a majority of students, faculty, and alumni, Greek associations were brought to the campus for the first time in 1954. Now, about half of TCU's undergraduates belong to nationally recognized chapters.

Aerial view of Worth Hills residence hall area, 1964
(courtesy Mary Couts Burnett Library).

The architecture in the dormitory area of Worth Hills is unremarkable. It continues the basic classical style set for dorms in 1942 with the construction of Foster Hall for women. Three of the buildings are rectangular; four are T-shaped. All retain the main campus tones of buff brick, red roof, and white cast-stone trim. The sororities, however, have added a touch of individualism and a splash of color by mounting over their entrance doors canvas canopies emblazoned with the Greek chapter letters. Architects Preston Geren and Joseph Pelich were responsible for the design of all the buildings in the dormitory group as well as the cafeteria building. All but two, Brachman Hall and Wiggins Hall, had been built by 1964.

One of the Worth Hills fraternity dormitories was named Tomlinson Hall, "In honor of [a] great and good family," as the dedication program reads. The Tomlinson name weaves in and out through the fabric of TCU history and its family members have provided incomparable strength and support from the early days of the century to the present. It was the T. E. Tomlinson branch of the family for whom the hall was named. T. E. Tomlinson was a member of the Board of Trustees from 1907 to 1941 and was chairman when the decision was made to move to Fort Worth. One of the first streets bordering the 1911 TCU campus was named Tomlinson Drive in his honor, but it has since been renamed Bellaire Drive North. For his good works and uncommon service, TCU awarded him an honorary doctorate in 1942. T. E.'s son, Clyde, was a TCU graduate and a trustee from 1946 to 1964. In 1964, while Clyde was acting chairman, the decision was made to adopt the first integration policy at the school. T. E.'s nephews Douglas, Roy, and Homer were also educated at the university. Douglas, publisher and founder of the All-Church Press, was a member of the Brite College Board of Trustees from 1943 to 1971; Beatrice, a sis-

ter, married Colby D. Hall. Tomlinson Hall is home
to the Kappa Sigma, Sigma Chi, Phi Delta Theta, and
Lambda Chi Alpha fraternities.

The second fraternity dorm, situated immediately
west of Tomlinson Hall, is named Martin-Moore after two TCU figures of long and successful tenure. A
TCU alumnus, Othol "Abe" Martin was the Frogs'
head football coach from 1953 through the 1966 season, continuing then as athletic director until his retirement in 1975. Known to friends and colleagues as
"Honest Abe," he led his teams to three Southwest
Conference titles in the '50s. One of the most
respected men in collegiate athletics, he was
presented with the 1968 Alonzo Stagg award, the
highest honor in the college coaching profession, by
the American Football Coaches Association.

Jerome A. Moore was in the service of the university as student, teacher, and administrator. A 1923
graduate of TCU and an ordained minister, Moore
was instructor of Spanish at Texas Woman's College
from 1928 to 1943. In 1943, he returned to his alma
mater to become the first dean of TCU's AddRan
College of Arts and Sciences, retiring from that post
in 1973 to become Dean Emeritus of the University.
During this time he also was professor of Spanish
and chairman of the modern language department, as
well as serving as secretary to the Board of Trustees
for twenty-five years. The highly esteemed Dean
Moore was awarded an honorary degree in 1968 by a
grateful TCU. Martin-Moore Hall houses Phi Kappa
Sigma, Phi Gamma Delta, Delta Tau Delta, and
Sigma Alpha Epsilon fraternities.

Beckham-Shelburne Hall is home to the Pi Beta
Phi, Chi Omega, Delta Gamma, and Kappa Alpha
Theta sororities. Sadie Beckham and Elizabeth Shelburne had a combined service of more than forty
years as deans of women at TCU. Mrs. Beckham began her tenure in 1920, first as matron of Jarvis Hall,
then as dean of women. Retiring in 1937, she passed

T. E. Tomlinson (courtesy Mary Couts Burnett Library).

Clyde Tomlinson (courtesy University Publications).

Othol "Abe" Martin (courtesy Sports Information Office).

Jerome A. Moore (courtesy University Publications).

Sadie T. Beckham (courtesy Mary Couts Burnett Library).

Elizabeth Shelburne (author's collection).

the reins to her assistant, Miss Shelburne, who served in that position until 1961. Mrs. Beckham was also the second woman to be elected a member of the Board of Trustees, being appointed to that post in 1937 and continuing through 1954, when she was made an honorary trustee. A TCU graduate, Miss Shelburne came back to the campus in 1929 as hostess in Jarvis Hall and instructor in math. Her tenure as dean of women spanned twenty-four years. Upon leaving that post, she was supervisor of the health facilities until her final retirement from active college life in 1968. Both women had the well-deserved respect and admiration of students and colleagues alike.

Moody Hall was named in honor of W. L. Moody, Jr., of Galveston who, with his wife, established a foundation in 1942 to assist religious, charitable, scientific, and educational organizations in Texas. On more than one occasion, the university has been a recipient of grants from the Moody Foundation. In dedicating the hall, then-Chancellor J. M. Moudy said, "TCU is fortunate to have been chosen as one of the places where the outstanding works of Mr. Moody will live after him." Moody, who was characterized as "quiet, retiring, and publicity shy," died in Galveston in 1954. Moody Hall provides space for Zeta Tau Alpha, Kappa Kappa Gamma, Alpha Chi Omega, and Delta Delta Delta sororities.

Two more sororities, Kappa Delta and Alpha Delta Pi are housed in Frances Sadler Hall. The smallest of the Worth Hills dormitories, it is named for the wife of M. E. Sadler, chief executive officer from 1941 to 1965. In the designation, TCU recognized the "dedicated and capable contribution which Mrs. Sadler had made to the appropriateness of new construction on the campus as well as to the life of the University in other ways." It was Mrs. Sadler who was singularly responsible for the interior design of the Carr Chapel. A woman of quiet dignity, she served as a strong and faithful First Lady. In ill health for many of her later years, Frances Sadler died in 1971.

Wiggins Hall and Brachman Hall complete the student accommodations on the Worth Hills campus. Mary Lipscomb Wiggins Hall, built in 1972, is the latest women's residence at TCU and is non-Greek. The lady after whom it is named was one of the ten members of the 1896 graduating class of what was known then as Add-Ran Christian University of Waco. Both of Mrs. Wiggins' daughters completed their degrees at TCU in Fort Worth. One of the daughters, Ruth, had a further tie to the university through her marriage to the late Judge A. D. Green, a TCU alumnus and member of the Board of Trustees. The $1.4 million Wiggins' estate was bequeathed in equal parts to the TCU and Brite College corporations. The Greens have also made significant contributions to the university in loyalty and financial support.

W. L. Moody, Jr. (courtesy
University Publications).

Frances Sadler (courtesy
Mary Couts Burnett
Library).

Mary Lipscomb Wiggins
(courtesy Mary Couts
Burnett Library).

Etta and Sol Brachman
(courtesy University
Publications).

Brachman Hall was constructed in 1970 as an "experimental" dormitory. It was designed as a modern
adaptation of the European tradition of the
"residential college" in which the ultimate emphasis
is on living and learning. Built in a T-shape, Brach-
133

man houses men in the north section and women in the south. Included in the unit are classrooms, seminar rooms, faculty offices and living quarters, and "common" rooms for coeducational study and social activity. Students who live in Brachman are involved in many of the same activities academically and socially. Called simply "New Hall" during its first year of operation, the building was officially dedicated and named the Solomon and Etta P. Brachman Hall in 1971. Brachman was a local businessman whose philanthropy was generously extended to TCU. In 1959, he was given honorary membership in the TCU Alumni Association and in 1968 he was awarded an honorary Doctor of Laws degree by the university. A bronze plaque inside the building recognizes the Brachman family, Dr. and Mrs. Malcolm K. Brachman and Marilyn Brachman Hoffman. Malcolm Brachman sat on the Board of Trustees from 1975 to 1990.

A pond lies south and west of Tomlinson and Martin-Moore dormitories, and on its far side there are a number of large white tanks within a fenced compound. This is the university's Experimental Mesocosm Facility, the purpose of which is to study factors that regulate plankton communities in Texas lakes and reservoirs. Through the study of lake fish and nutrients, species composition of plankton can be ascertained. Under the local direction of Dr. Ray Drenner, TCU biology professor, the research is funded by the National Science Foundation, the Texas Water Resources Institute, the FMC Corporation, and the TCU Research Foundation. Further, the Tarrant County Water Control District funds research on water quality. Each of the thirty fiberglass tanks holds 1500 gallons and is equipped with airlift systems for circulation. The nearby mobile unit is a laboratory especially designed for the Environmental Protection Agency by the late Dr. Clifford

Murphy of TCU. Brought to TCU from its original location in the Houston ship channel, the facility is one of only three such in the world.

Directly north of the tanks and west of Brachman Hall is the main office building of the TCU Physical Plant Department. Farther west is the Mary Potishman Lard Tennis Center.

TENNIS CENTER

The Tennis Center, located at 3609 Bellaire Drive North, was a gift to the university and to the tennis-playing community by the Mary Potishman Lard Trust of Fort Worth. Designed by Jack Kamrath of MacKie and Kamrath Architects of Houston in consultation with the Tennis Planning Consultants of Houston and Chicago, the center was sculpted out of the natural hill-and-valley land formation of the Worth Hills property. It is, perhaps, the most picturesque setting on the entire campus.

Approaching along the curving entrance walkway that leads into the center, one is afforded a nice view of the TCU campus eastward, with the spire of Carr Chapel visible over the red roof of Reed Hall. The beautifully manicured grounds, which include picnic and playground areas for patrons and their families, are maintained as a part of the gift from the Lard Trust.

Ranked among the top twenty-five facilities in the country by the United States Tennis Association, the center has five indoor and twenty-two outdoor courts. All outdoor courts are recessed for better wind protection and visibility. Six courts reserved primarily for the TCU varsity tennis program and for championship tournaments are provided with stadium seating for 1350 spectators.

Mary Potishman Lard Tennis Center, about 1976 (courtesy University Publications).

At the heart of the center, on the mall between the outdoor courts, is the Pro Shop in which are located the locker rooms, a varsity classroom, and the office of tennis coach "Tut" Bartzen, a former collegiate and USTA champion who has been the only director of the center since its opening in 1976. In addition, a retail shop offers a complete line of tennis equipment, apparel, and accessories. Around the walls of the retail shop are pictures representing the tennis teams' accomplishments in collegiate competition — a TCU Tennis Hall of Fame.

The tennis complex is named after Mary Potishman Lard, a member of the prominent Potishman family of Fort Worth who continue to be strong sup-

Aerial view of the Tennis Center, 1976 (courtesy University Publications).

porters of and benefactors to the university. The tennis facility associated with the Rickel Center was earlier provided by her brother, Leo Potishman. A nephew and former mayor of Fort Worth, Bayard Friedman, serves as executor of the Mary Potishman Lard Trust. He was instrumental in establishing the tennis mecca that is unique in offering use of its facilities to both the campus and the community, effectively bringing "town and gown" together. Friedman has been a member of the TCU Board of Trustees since 1971 and was chairman from 1979 to 1990. A long-time tennis enthusiast, he is a center "regular."

Epilogue

You have now visited the final location on this tour of Texas Christian University. Whether you followed from the outset or joined in along the way, it is hoped that the journey was pleasant and informative, and that you will take away with you some small part of the spirit that shaped the past and is guiding the present of this institution of teaching and learning.

Long years have been covered in this account, which has required a brevity that necessarily fragments significant times and foreshortens individual lives. It would be unseemly and sad to dismiss or take for granted the hardships, sacrifice, passion, strain, weariness, vision, despair, jubilation, dedication, commitment, and wonder that was theirs. May their lives and deeds not be diminished or ignored, but held up as a light for our path into the future.

Appendices

ARCHITECTS

(Parenthetical dates indicate either original construction, later renovation or expansion.)

Carter and Burgess
Landscape architects for much of the campus, including the Athletic Complex and the Worth Hills campus
W. G. Clarkson
Mary Couts Burnett Library (1925)
University Christian Church (1933, 1951)
Preston Geren
Bailey Building (1958)
Bass Building

Brachman Hall
Brown-Lupton Health Center
Brown-Lupton Student Center
Clark Hall (1958)
Colby Hall Dormitory
Martin-Moore Hall
M. E. Sadler Hall
Tomlinson Hall
University Christian Church (1965)
Worth Hills Cafeteria
Wyatt C. Hedrick
Dan D. Rogers Hall
Amon G. Carter Stadium (1930)
Hedrick, Geren, and Pelich
Foster Hall

Landreth Hall
Mary Couts Burnett Library (1958, with Stanley as associate)
Pete Wright Hall
Tom Brown Hall
Waits Hall
Winton-Scott Hall
Jack Kamrath (McKie as consultant)
Mary Potishman Lard Tennis Center
Kirk, Voich, Gist
Tandy Hall
Albert Komatsu
Miller Speech-Hearing Clinic
Moncrief Hall
Dan D. Rogers Hall (1977)
Starpoint School
Joseph Pelich
Beckham-Shelburne Hall
Daniel-Meyer Coliseum
Frances Sadler Hall
Milton Daniel Hall
Religion Center (Brite, Beasley, Carr Chapel)
Reed Hall (1961)
Rickel Building
Sherley Hall
W. L. Moody Hall
Wiggins Hall
Kevin Roche
Moudy Building
Paul Rudolph
Sid W. Richardson Building
Sanguinet & Staats
Brite College of the Bible (1914)
Skidmore, Owings, and Merrill (Walter Netsch, principal)
Mary Couts Burnett Library (1982)
Van Slyke & Woodruff
Memorial Arch (1923)
Gymnasium (1921)
Waller & Field
Jarvis Hall (1911)
Administration Building (1911)
Clark Hall (1912)
Goode Hall (1911)

CHRONOLOGICAL BUILDING SEQUENCE OF MAJOR STRUCTURES

1911
Administration Building (renovated 1961, named Dave Reed Hall)
Jarvis Hall girls' dormitory (renovated 1955)
Goode Hall ministerial and boys' dormitory
1912

Clark Hall boys' dormitory

1914
Brite College of the Bible (renovated 1958, renamed Bailey Building)

1921
Gymnasium

1923
Memorial Arch

1925
Mary Couts Burnett Library (enlarged 1958, 1982)

1930
Stadium west (enlarged, 1948, named Amon Carter Stadium; enlarged, 1953, 1956)

1933
University Christian Church

1942
Foster Hall women's dormitory

1947
Tom Brown Hall men's dormitory

1948
Waits Hall women's dormitory
Stadium east

1949
Fine Arts Building/Ed Landreth Auditorium

1952
Winton-Scott Hall of Science

1953
Religion center begun; complex contains Brite Divinity School, Beasley Undergraduate Religion, and Robert Carr Chapel

1955
Brown-Lupton Student Center
Pete Wright Hall boys' dormitory
Jarvis Hall renovated

1956
Upper deck, stadium

1957
Colby Hall women's dormitory
Milton Daniel Hall men's dormitory
Dan D. Rogers Hall

1958
Sherley Hall women's dormitory
Clark Hall men's dormitory (new Clark Hall)
Mary Couts Burnett Library enlarged
Brite College renovated, renamed Bailey Building
Original Goode Hall demolished

1959
Original Clark Hall demolished

1960
Sadler Hall administration building

1961
Daniel-Meyer Coliseum
Ames Observatory
Administration Building
renovated, named
Reed Hall

1963
Brown-Lupton Health
Center

1964
Worth Hills campus ac-
quired; four residence
halls built:
Beckham-Shelburne
Hall sorority house
Frances Sadler Hall so-
rority house
W. L. Moody Hall soror-
ity house
Tomlinson Hall frater-
nity house

1965
Martin-Moore Hall fra-
ternity house
Worth Hills cafeteria

1970
Brachman Hall coed
dormitory

1971
Sid W. Richardson Phys-
ical Sciences Building
Annie Richardson Bass
Building

1972
Cyrus K. and Ann
Rickel Building
Mary Lipscomb Wiggins
Hall women's dormi-
tory

1973
Gymnasium renovated,
becomes Ballet Build-
ing

1975
Miller Speech-Hearing
Clinic

1976
Mary Potishman Lard
Tennis Center

1978
Starpoint School

1982
James M. Moudy Visual
and Communications
Arts Building
Mary Couts Burnett Li-
brary addition

1988
Moncrief Hall dormitory
(coed)

1989
Tandy Hall

1992
Ranch Management
building

Bibliography

BOOKS

Clark, Joseph Lynn. *Thank God We Made It!: a Family Affair with Education.* Austin: University of Texas, Humanities Research Center, 1969.

Clark, Randolph. *Reminiscences: Biographical and Historical.* Wichita Falls, Texas: Lee Clark, Publisher, 1919; reprinted Texas Christian University Press, 1986.

Colquitt, Betsy. *Prologue: the TCU Library to 1983.* Fort Worth: Mary Couts Burnett Library, 1983.

Corder, Jim W., with photographs by Michael Chesser and Linda Kaye. *More Than a Century.* Fort Worth: Texas Christian University Press, 1973.

Flemmons, Jerry. *Amon. the Life of Amon Carter, Sr. of Texas.* Austin: Jenkins Publishing Co., 1978.

Fort Worth: Upper North, Northeast, East, Far South, and Far West. Tarrant County Historic Resources Survey. Fort Worth: Historic Preservation Council for Tarrant County, Texas, 1989.

Hall, Colby D. *The Early Years: University Christian Church, Fort Worth,*

Texas, 1873 – 1941. Published by the Church, 1983.

_____. *History of Texas Christian University: a College of the Cattle Frontier.* Fort Worth: Texas Christian University Press, 1947.

_____. "Source Material and Memoranda in Connection With the History of Texas Christian University, A College of the Cattle Frontier." 2 vols. unpublished, ca. 1941, Special Collections, TCU Library.

Hammond, John H. *Jerome A. Moore: a Man of TCU.* Fort Worth: Texas Christian University Press, 1974.

Harris, Lucy. *The Harris College of Nursing: Five Decades of Struggle for a Cause.* Fort Worth: Texas Christian University Press, 1973.

Hartley, Julia Magee. *Old American Glass: the Mills Collection at Texas Christian University.* Fort Worth: Texas Christian University Press, 1975.

Keith, Noel L. *The Brites of Capote.* Fort Worth: Texas Christian University Press, 1950.

Knight, Oliver, and Cissy Stewart Lale. *Fort Worth: Outpost on the Trinity.* Fort Worth: Texas Christian University Press, 1990.

Mason, Mrs. Frank Miller. "The Beginnings of Texas Christian University." Unpublished Master's Thesis. Texas Christian University, 1930.

Monroe, "Cowboy" Louis. *The Life Story of "Cowboy" Louis Monroe.* Privately published, 1968.

Moore, Jerome A. *Texas Christian University: a Hundred Years of History.* Fort Worth: Texas Christian University Press, 1973.

Pirtle, Caleb. *Fort Worth: the Civilized West.* Tulsa, Oklahoma: Continental Heritage Press, 1980.

Starpoint, A Shining Place, (for the Dedication of Starpoint School) Fort Worth: Texas Christian University Press, 1978.

Van Zandt, K. M. *Force Without Fanfare: the Autobiography of K. M. Van Zandt.* Edited and with an Introduction by Sandra L. Myres. Fort Worth: Texas Christian University Press, 1968.

ARTICLES

Kerner, Sarah Normand. "Sharing a 115-Room Home Sweet Home," *This Is TCU,* Vol. 34, No. 1 (March, 1991), pp. 8 – 9.

Pattie, Jane. "The Brite Legacy," *The Cattleman,* (March, 1990).

Simpson, D. Dwayne. "Saul B. Sells (1913 – 1988)," *American Psychologist,* Vol. 43, No. 12 (1988), p. 1088.

Swaim, Joan Hewatt. "Fenestration," *Windows: the Library Newsletter*, Vol. 1, No. 2 (December, 1988), pp. 5 – 7.

_____. "A Homecoming," *This Is TCU*, Vol. 31, No. 4 (December, 1988), p. 30.

_____. "Of Time and the Drag," *This Is TCU*, Vol. 33, No. 3 (September, 1990), p. 38.

_____. "Putting Things Back Where They Belong," *This Is TCU*, Vol. 29, No. 2 (May, 1987), pp. 38 – 39.

_____. "A Space That Holds Time — and All That Stuff," *This Is TCU*, Vol. 31, No. 3 (October 1988), p. 38.

_____. "A TCU Cowboy," *This Is TCU*, Vol. 30, No.1 (March, 1988), pp. 38 – 39.

_____. "They Still Teach Shakespeare, Don't They?" *This Is TCU*, Vol. 34, No. 2 (May, 1991), p. 38.

_____. "The Wildflower Field," *This Is TCU*, Vol. 30, No. 2 (May, 1988), p. 38.

Thistlethwaite, Mark. "'TCU Style' and Architecture," *This Is TCU*, Vol. 25, No. 4 (April, 1983), pp. 5 – 7, 10.

Westrate, Linda J. "Names on a Plaque," unpublished paper presented as an entry in TCU's Creative Writing Contest, January 28, 1988.

PAMPHLETS

Brite Divinity School: An historical sketch. [Compiled by Joseph R. Jeter, Jr.]. Published by Brite Divinity School, Texas Christian University, 1989.

Clark, Randolph. "Sketch of the Life of Elder J. A. Clark." Unpublished, ca. 1920, TCU Library.

Dedication: Cyrus K. and Ann C. Rickel Building for Health, Physical Education and Recreation, Texas Christian University. Program of Events, October 12, 1972.

IBR/TCU: Institute of Behavioral Research at Texas Christian University, 1991.

Rec Sports: Do It Your Way! Department of Recreational Sports, Texas Christian University, 1991.

Waits, Edward McShane. *The Dedication of Foster Hall.* 1943.

Yearning to Know. Starpoint School, 1990.

ADDITIONAL RESOURCES

Fort Worth Star-Telegram.

The Horned Frog. Annual of Texas Christian University.

The Skiff. A weekly newspaper published under the auspices of the student body of Texas Christian University.

The Skiff. 1980 – 1991. A daily newspaper published under the auspices of the student body of Texas Christian University.

TCU News Service releases.

Texas Christian University

Bulletin: Graduate Studies, 1989 – 90/1990 – 91. Vol. 83, No. 2, April 1989.

Texas Christian University Bulletin: Undergraduate Studies, 1991/1992 – 1992/1993. Vol. 85, No. 1, March 1991.

Files in the Special Collections Department, Mary Couts Burnett Library, Texas Christian University.

Index

152